Incredible iPad™ Apps

FOR

DUMMIES®

by Bob LeVitus
with Bryan Chaffin

WILEY

Wiley Publishing, Inc.

Incredible iPad™ Apps For Dummies®

Published by
Wiley Publishing, Inc.
111 River Street
Hoboken, NJ 07030-5774
www.wiley.com

WILEY

About the Authors

Bob LeVitus, often referred to as "Dr. Mac," has written or co-written nearly 60 popular tech books, including *iPhone For Dummies,* 4th Edition, *Mac OS X Snow Leopard For Dummies,* and *Dr. Mac: The OS X Files* for Wiley Publishing, Inc.; *Stupid Mac Tricks* and *Dr. Macintosh* for Addison-Wesley; and *The Little iTunes Book* and *The Little iDVD Book* for Peachpit Press. His books have sold more than a million copies worldwide.

Bob pens the popular "Dr. Mac" column for the *Houston Chronicle* (and has since 1966) and has been published in dozens of computer magazines in several countries over his 25-year career as a tech writer.

In his copious spare time, Bob heads up a team of expert technical consultants who do nothing but provide technical help and training to Mac users via telephone, e-mail, and/or their unique Internet-enabled remote-control software, which allows the team to see and control your Mac no matter where in the world you may be. If you're having problems with your Mac, you ought to give them a try. You'll find them at www.boblevitus.com or 408-627-7577.

Prior to giving his life over to computers, Bob spent years at Kresser/Craig/D.I.K. (a Los Angeles advertising agency and marketing consultancy) and its subsidiary, L & J Research. He holds a B.S. in Marketing from California State University.

At the end of the day, Bob is best known for his expertise, trademark humorous style, and ability to translate techie jargon into usable and fun advice for regular folks.

Bryan Chaffin is the cofounder, copublisher, and sometime editor of *The Mac Observer* at www.macobserver.com, where he has pontificated at length about all things Apple for more than thirteen years. He also cohosts *The Apple Context Machine* podcast with Jeff Gamet, and can often be heard on the *MacVoices* and *MacJury* podcasts (just listen for the word "Balderdash!" being yelled out and that's likely him).

In addition to his online work at *TMO,* Bryan has contributed to *MacAddict* and *MacFormat* magazines, and he was pleased-as-punch to tech edit *GarageBand For Dummies* for Bob LeVitus, as well as to contribute to *Incredible iPhone Apps For Dummies.*

Most recently he penned the "Must Have Apps" section of *iPad All-In-One For Dummies*, by Nancy Muir.

Though Apple has consumed his professional life since Bill Clinton was president, Bryan also loves music. He is lucky enough to play guitar in The Macworld All Stars with Bob and some other great Mac people, and one of the achievements of which he is most proud is having recorded the album *Let It Burn* as part of The Atomic Love Bombs in 2009. He is currently in the process of putting together a new band even as he writes this.

Dedication

Bob: This book is dedicated to my wife of more than 25 years, the lovely Lisa, who taught me almost everything I know about almost everything I know that's not made by Apple, Inc. And to my children, Allison and Jacob, who love their iPhones almost as much as I love them (the kids, not their iPhones).

Bryan: I'd like to dedicate this book to my business partner, Dave Hamilton, for all his hard work and friendship at *The Mac Observer* over the years. In addition to being the best drummer East of The Mississippi, Dave has done an incredible job of making *The Mac Observer* a viable business all these years.

Authors' Acknowledgments

Big-time thanks to the gang at Wiley: Bob "Is the damn thing done yet?" Woerner, Pat "Low Key" O'Brien, Andy "Big Boss Man" Cummings, Barry "Still no humorous nickname" Pruett, and anyone and everyone else at Wiley who was involved in any way with bringing this book to market.

Bob: An extra-super-special great big thank you goes to Bryan Chaffin. Not only did he pitch in when I really needed help, he was a pleasure to work with and an all-around great guy I'm proud to call my friend.

Thanks also to super-agent Carole "Swifty" Jelen, for doing what she does best. You've represented me for over 20 years, Carole; I hope you'll represent me for at least 20 more.

Eternal gratitude to my family and friends, for putting up with me during my all-too lengthy absences while this book was gestating. And big-time thanks to Saccone's Pizza, Rudy's BBQ, Taco Cabana, the Soda-Club System, and HEB for sustenance.

Bryan: I hate to turn the Acknowledgments section into some kind of big mutual admiration society, but I simply have to thank Bob LeVitus for all the help and friendship he has offered me over the years! He has given me more opportunities than I could tell you about, and he has been an amazing mentor from the moment we first met.

I'd also like to thank Jeff Gamet, Managing Editor of *The Mac Observer*, for his help throughout this project. From showing me some cool iPad apps to covering the news desk for me after an all-nighter *For Dummies* writing session, Jeff has had my back every step of the way!

And of course, I have to thank my mother for all her help and support along the way – thanks, Mom!

Bob & Bryan (in unison): And finally, thanks to you, gentle reader, for buying this book.

Publisher's Acknowledgments

We're proud of this book; please send us your comments at http://dummies.custhelp.com. For other comments, please contact our Customer Care Department within the U.S. at 877-762-2974, outside the U.S. at 317-572-3993, or fax 317-572-4002.

Some of the people who helped bring this book to market include the following:

Acquisitions, Editorial

Project Editor: Pat O'Brien

Acquisitions Editor: Bob Woerner

Senior Copy Editor: Barry Childs-Helton

Editorial Manager: Kevin Kirschner

Editorial Assistant: Amanda Graham

Sr. Editorial Assistant: Cherie Case

Cartoons: Rich Tennant (www.the5thwave.com)

Composition Services

Project Coordinator: Kristie Rees

Layout and Graphics: Carrie A. Cesavice, Erin Zeltner

Proofreaders: Lindsay Littrell, Christine Sabooni

Publishing and Editorial for Technology Dummies

Richard Swadley, Vice President and Executive Group Publisher

Andy Cummings, Vice President and Publisher

Mary Bednarek, Executive Acquisitions Director

Mary C. Corder, Editorial Director

Publishing for Consumer Dummies

Diane Graves Steele, Vice President and Publisher

Composition Services

Debbie Stailey, Director of Composition Services

Cover Credits

Air Display © Avatron Software, Inc.
Bill Atkinson PhotoCard © Bill Atkinson Photography
Bloom HD © Opal Limited
Calculator XL © Luke Campbell
Comics © Iconology, Inc.
Corkulous © Appigo, Inc.
EyeTV © Elgato Systems
Flight Track Pro © Mobiata LLC
GoodReader © Good.iWare
Marquee © Yodel Code

Motion X GPS Drive © Fullpower Technologies, Inc.
OmniGraffle © The Omni Group
PrintCentral © EuroSmartz Ltd.
Prompster © Danté Varnado Moore
SoundNote © David Estes
StockSpy HD © Calvin Schut
Things © Cultured Code
Uzu © Jason K. Smith
Wikihood © Stephan Gillmeier
Zen Timer © Spotlight Six Software

Table of Contents

Chapter 7: Games 78

Chapter 8: Healthcare & Fitness 90

Chapter 9: Music... 102

Chapter 13: Social Networking....................... 150

Chapter 14: Travel, Navigation, and Weather... 162

Chapter 15: Utilities... 174

Chapter 16: Miscellaneous 186

Introduction

*L*et me get one thing out of the way right from the get-go: I think you're pretty darn smart for buying a *For Dummies* book. That says to me that you have the confidence and intelligence to know what you don't know. The *For Dummies* franchise is built around the core notion that all of us feel insecure about certain topics when tackling them for the first time, especially when those topics have to do with technology.

And speaking of "Dummies," remember that it's just a word. I don't think you're dumb — quite the opposite! And for what it's worth, I asked if we could leave "Dummies" out of the title and call it something like, *Incredible iPad Apps For People Smart Enough to Know They Couldn't Possibly Evaluate Thousands of iPad Apps and Live to Tell About It.* My editors just laughed. "C'mon, that's the whole point of the name!" they insisted. "And besides, it's shorter our way."

Sigh.

About This Book

This, my 58th technical book, was, along with *Incredible iPhone Apps For Dummies*, one of the hardest books I've had to write. Yet I think I had more fun writing it (and *Incredible iPhone Apps For Dummies*) than any of the others and here's why. . . .

Thousands upon thousands of iPad apps are available in the App Store with thousands more added each month. No single human (or even a rather large *team* of humans) could look at them all, much less give every one of them a thorough workout.

So my first challenge was to narrow the field to a manageable size. I began by looking for apps that had achieved some measure of acclaim, a combination of iTunes Store ranking, positive buzz on the Web, iTunes Store reviews, the opinions of friends and colleagues who matter (you know who you are), the opinions of my family, the opinions of the many enthusiastic iPad fans at Wiley Publishing, reviews in print, and reviews on the Web. Then I added the thousands of dollars' worth of apps already in my personal collection. When all was said and done, I had around 300 apps that were contenders, and I spent several months testing them, taking notes, and capturing screen shots.

My next challenge was figuring out how many categories (chapters) should be included and which ones they should be. This was almost as hard as determining the 300+ contenders. But after much deliberation and consideration, I decided that there would be 16 incredible-apps chapters plus 3 bonus "top ten" chapters. Furthermore, Chapter 16 would be called "Misc." and contain the apps that didn't fit elsewhere in the book.

Deciding on the number of apps that would appear in each chapter was easier: I suggested ten and nobody argued, so that was that.

Selecting the 160 most incredible apps (16 chapters × 10 apps) was incredibly difficult, as was deciding where each app belonged. Many apps could just as easily fit in one chapter as another. *Merriam-Webster's Collegiate Dictionary* app, for example, ended up in the Reference chapter but would have been equally at home in the Book-Related or News and Info chapters. The Bloom HD app appears in the Music chapter, but should I have put it in Art & Artistry? Don't even get me started on Business, Utility, and Productivity apps. It was impossible, so in the end, I just went with my heart.

Then, realizing it might take me months to write about the 160+ apps that made the final cut, I enlisted the help of my friend and colleague Bryan Chaffin, executive vice president and opinion columnist and podcaster for *The Mac Observer* and an iPad app geek just like me. I gave him the 8 chapters I wanted least and granted him free rein to overrule my picks in his chapters. If you're keeping score, Bryan wrote Chapters 3 (Business), 5 (Finance), 6 (Food, Cooking, and Nutrition), 8 (Healthcare and Fitness), 10 (News and Info), 12 (Reference), 13 (Social Networking), and 16 (Misc.). And I wrote Chapters 1 (Art and Artistry), 2 (Book-Related Apps), 4 (Entertainment), 7 (Games), 9 (Music), 11 (Productivity), 14 (Travel, Navigation, and Weather), and 15 (Utilities). I also wrote the three top-ten lists in Chapters 17–19.

If you really think we put an app in the wrong chapter, just know that we did the best we could at an impossible task and take some pity on us. Or drop us a note — our contact info appears at the end this chapter.

How This Book Is Organized

While we're on the subject of chapters, here's something we imagine you've never heard before: Most books have a beginning, a middle, and an end. Generally, you do well to adhere to that linear structure — unless you're one of those knuckleheads out to ruin it for the rest of us by jumping ahead and revealing that the butler did it.

Fortunately, there is no ending to spoil in a *For Dummies* book. So although you may want to digest this book from start to finish — and we hope you do — we won't penalize you for skipping ahead or jumping around. Having said that, we organized *Incredible iPad Apps For Dummies* and the contents of each chapter in the order we think makes the most sense — alphabetical.

So the first 15 chapters are organized from *A* to *Z*, followed by Chapter 16 (Miscellaneous).

Each chapter in the book contains five apps, listed alphabetically, each getting two full pages of description and pictures. These five apps are followed by five more apps, also alphabetized, with shorter descriptions. The five apps with the longer descriptions and pictures were selected only because we felt those were the apps that would benefit most from longer descriptions and pictures. The five apps with shorter descriptions and no pictures were the ones we felt we could describe adequately in a paragraph or two.

Please understand that the apps are not ranked in any way within the chapter. Ranking the apps #1 through #10 was more than we could bear; just think of the ten apps in each chapter as more or less equally incredible.

Last, but not least, you'll find three chapters at the end with top-ten lists styled after the chapters found in "The Part of Tens" in a regular *For Dummies book* — think of it as the *For Dummies* answer to David Letterman. The lists presented in Chapters 17 and 18 steer you to my favorite free and paid iPad apps. If you read this book from cover to cover, you'll already know about the apps I discuss in Chapters 17 and 18 — because they are, after all, my favorites. But I try not to repeat myself. Instead, I explain why each app made the cut — and offer some tips or discuss some additional features of each app. The final top-ten list, in Chapter 19, offers my suggestions for some essential iPad peripherals and accessories you might want to consider adding.

Conventions Used in This Book

First, we want to tell you how we go about our business. *Incredible iPad Apps For Dummies* makes generous use of bullet lists and pictures. And all Web and e-mail addresses are shown in a special monofont typeface, `like this`.

There are no links to the App Store because they're long and easy to mistype. Rather, we took great pains to ensure that all app names are properly spelled, so you should have no trouble finding them using the App Store's search engine.

We've listed prices for each app, and these prices were accurate at the time this book was printed. That said, developers change App prices regularly, so the price you see in the book may not be the same as the price you see in the App Store. Rest assured, it was right when this book went to press — and if it's not right anymore, please blame (or thank) the developer.

Icons Used in This Book

Little round pictures (icons) appear in the left margins throughout this book. Consider these icons miniature road signs, telling you something extra about the topic at hand or hammering a point home.

Here's what the three icons used in this book look like and mean.

These are the juicy morsels, shortcuts, and recommendations that might make the task at hand faster or easier.

This icon emphasizes the stuff we think you ought to retain. You may even jot down a note to yourself in the iPad.

You wouldn't intentionally run a stop sign, would you? In the same fashion, ignoring warnings may be hazardous to your iPad and (by extension) your wallet. There, you now know how these warning icons work: You have just received your very first warning!

Good news! This app is compatible with both the iPad and the iPhone!

A Note about Project Gutenberg

Most books published in the United States prior to 1923 are considered to be in the *public domain*. This means they are free of copyright and that anyone can print them, distribute them electronically, or even charge money for them. Project Gutenberg (www.gutenberg.org) is the first and largest single collection of free electronic books (*e-books*) on the Web today, with more than 30,000 free books. We mention Project Gutenberg and its plethora of titles several times in these pages. Now you know what I'm referring to.

Where to Go from Here

Why, straight to Chapter 1, of course (without passing Go). But first, there's one more thing:

We didn't write this book for ourselves. We wrote it for you, gentle reader. And we would love to hear how it worked for you. So please send us your thoughts, platitudes, likes and dislikes, and any other comments. You can send us snail-mail in care of Wiley, but that takes a really, really long time to reach us and we don't have time to respond to most of it anyway. If you want a response, your best bet is to send e-mail to us directly at

    incredibleiphoneapps@boblevitus.com

or

    bryan2@macobserver.com

We appreciate your feedback, and we *try* to respond to all reasonably polite e-mail within a few days.

Last, but not least, let us make you an offer you can't refuse: If you know of an app you think should appear in the next edition of this book, please send me (Bob) an e-mail message explaining why you think so and the chapter you think it belongs in. If I like the app enough to include it in the next edition of this book, I'll not only thank you in the Acknowledgments section, I'll also send you a free auto-graphed copy of the book. You've got to love that!

Okay, that's all we've got for now. Go — enjoy the book!

1 Art and Artistry

Art Authority for iPad
$8.99

Having Art Authority is like having the history of Western art in pictures and words on your iPad. The app includes works by hundreds of artists, organized alphabetically by artist and also by periods (called Rooms within the app) that include Early (up to the 1400s), Baroque, Renaissance, Romanticism, Impressionism, Modern, Contemporary, and American.

Tap one of these eight Rooms on the main screen and you'll see its subcategories; tap a subcategory and you can select a specific artist or an overview of that artist's work. The figure on the left below, for example, shows some of the subcategories in the Modern room, as well as the overlay for the Symbolism category.

If you prefer to see the bigger picture (ha!), tap a Room's name (Modern in the figure on the left below) instead of tapping a subcategory, and you can view the major works and timelines for that period.

Regardless of how you choose to explore the art — alphabetically or by period — you can find a dozen or more works by each artist arranged in a *Show*.

Art Authority offers myriad options for viewing Shows. You can choose your favorite transition or allow the app to select an appropriate one. You can turn on the Ken Burns effect to provide the illusion of motion. You can view thumbnails of all the artwork in a show, and tap individual thumbnails to see the pictures. You can speed up, slow down, stop, or reverse the show at any time, and you can enlarge, shrink, or rotate any picture. You can turn captions on or off, or display them briefly when a picture first appears. You can add music from your iTunes music library to any show, or you can delete any image and never see it again.

That's not all, though. You can also save any image from the app to your iPad's Photos app — or set any image as your wallpaper background. Another option lets you link from any image to the Web site from which it originated; there you can read additional facts and see other images. Of course, Art Authority also includes detailed information about each artist, as shown in the figure on the right. For what it's worth, the text you see in the figure is merely the first of 31 pages of information about Rembrandt.

Best features

Art Authority is beautiful, flexible, scholarly, and fun. If you like to look at art or learn about it, you'll find an ample supply of quality artwork and information in Art Authority.

Worst features

Because all the images are pulled from Web sites, the app is more or less useless if you don't have Internet access. Some pictures load slowly or don't load at all, depending upon Web traffic and the originating site's status, although this shortcoming isn't the fault of Art Authority.

To be fair, when you first view a picture, it's cached on your iPad, which makes it available at a later date even if you don't have Internet access.

Brushes
$7.99

Brushes is a drawing and painting app designed exclusively for the iPad. With a simple, elegant user interface, Brushes offers a powerful toolset for drawing and painting.

Thoughtful touches abound in Brushes. Tap once anywhere on the screen to show or hide the toolbar. Zoom in as much as 1,600% or out to 70% with the customary iPad pinch and unpinch gestures. Pick a color with a single press of your fingertip.

The app is called Brushes, so the obvious place to start exploring is with the brush styles, as shown in the figure on the left below. The app has more than a dozen types — smooth, fine-bristle, rough-bristle, ragged, and many more — which are available in any size from 1 to 64 pixels and offer complete control over the opacity of your strokes.

There's a terrific color picker (shown in the figure on the right below). To change the hue and saturation of the color you want to use for painting, drag the knob (a little white circle) around on the color wheel. Below the color wheel are two sliders. The top slider determines the brightness of the selected color; the bottom slider determines the color's opacity.

Many desktop graphics programs have an eyedropper tool to "pick up" any color in your image and paint with it. There's an eyedropper in the Brushes toolbar, too, but I almost always use the shortcut of pressing my finger in one spot for half a second, which causes the eyedropper tool to pop up directly under my fingertip.

Another cool feature of Brushes is its support for up to six layers. I've seen layers in many desktop graphics programs, but Brushes is one of only a few iPad apps that do layers and do them well. Each layer can be painted independently without affecting the layers above or below. You drag and drop to change the stacking order of the layers, which I find both elegant and intuitive. You have full control over layer opacity, so you can use a semitransparent layer to tint all or part of the layer(s) below. And you can merge any of the layers with any other(s) at any time.

Don't worry if you make a mistake — Brushes has at least ten levels of undo and redo, so you can undo or redo your last ten (or more) actions.

When you're finished with your masterpiece, you can save it in the Brushes gallery so you can easily work on it some more or show it to your friends with Brushes' built-in slideshow. You can export finished pictures to your iPad's Photos app or use the Brushes built-in Web server to view or download your creations over Wi-Fi with any Web browser on any Web-connected computer.

If you're a Mac OS X user, there's a cool free Brushes Viewer that lets you view or export high-resolution versions of your paintings on your Mac. Another interesting feature is that the Brushes Viewer can display a stroke-by-stroke animated replay of the making of your painting, which you can export as a QuickTime movie. Plus, the Brushes Viewer can export paintings at higher resolution (1,920 x 2,880 pixels) than the iPad screen (1,024 x 768).

Best features

The best feature of Brushes is its simple-but-powerful user interface. If you're artistically inclined, there's no limit to the things you can create with Brushes.

Worst features

The way-cool Brushes Viewer isn't available for Windows.

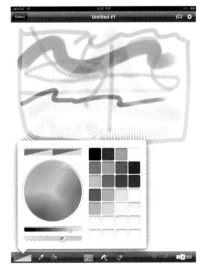

Color Splash for iPad
$1.99

Some photography apps are like a Swiss Army Knife, with bells, whistles, and features galore. Others, such as Color Splash, focus on doing one thing well. In this case, that one thing is converting a photo to black and white and then enabling you to colorize specific parts of it. Because a picture is worth a thousand words, I could technically tell you to check out the pictures below and move on to the next app.

Never fear, gentle reader; I vowed to tell you what you need to know. Even though that pair of pix says it all, let me tell you how the app works and how easy it is to achieve stunning effects.

Start with a picture. Any picture. In the figures below I started with an HDR (High Dynamic Range) shot I took of an Austin sunset over Lady Bird Lake. When you open a picture in Color Splash, it's converted to black and white automatically. Next it's time to get creative and break out one of the two brushes, called Color and Gray. The Color brush brushes away the black and white to reveal the colors in the original photo. The Gray brush does the opposite — it brushes away color you've revealed with the Color brush, which is handy if you make a mistake or want to zoom in to clean up problem areas.

And tapping the Brush button gives you total control over the size and strength of the paintbrush (that is, your fingertip). Your paintbrushes can be any size, from pencil-thin to fatter than my thumb. You can adjust the brush's opacity from nearly transparent to pretty much opaque. In sum, the brush controls are designed to make precision finger-painting easy. And finally, you can undo and redo brush strokes to your heart's content.

Check out the App Store listing for Color Splash and you'll see a few really stunning examples of the effect done well.

If you make a mistake, double-tap anywhere on the screen and the brush will switch from Color to Gray. Double-tap again and it changes back. It's fast, easy, and one of the most useful shortcuts I've seen in an app.

Tapping the little red dot at the top of the screen shows you the areas you've brushed with the Color brush by displaying them on screen in bright red, as shown in the figure on the left below.

The picture on the right shows my finished Color Splash picture. As you can see, in both images I used the Color brush to reveal the colors in the sky and sunset at the top of the image and the pool and chairs at the bottom. Everything else in the picture — basically the entire middle section — remains black and white.

The bottom line is that if a talentless clod like me can achieve stunning (in my humble opinion) artistic effects with Color Splash, just think what you'll be able to do.

Best features

With Color Splash you can create a unique and interesting effect with little effort or talent. It's actually kind of fun and the results are often stunning.

Worst features

There is sometimes a little bit of lag when you are painting. When it happens, it can affect your precision. Luckily, there are unlimited undos.

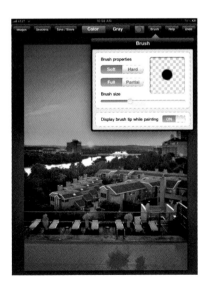

Photogene for iPad
$3.99

Photogene is one of my favorite apps. It's the app I use most often when I need to improve a photo I shot with my iPhone. It has most (if not all) the features I need to make a mediocre photo look good or to make a good photo look great.

Photogene has an exceptional user interface, with controls that are easier to understand and use than those of some other photo apps. Photogene also has an extensive list of features, represented by the icons at the bottom of the screen (as shown in the figures):

- ✔ **Scissors:** This cropping tool provides several preset aspect ratios, including 1:1 (square), 3:4 and 4:3 (standard rectangular photos), 9:16 (widescreen), and 3:2 (iPhone screen).

- ✔ **Arrows:** This icon has tools for rotating, flipping, or straightening your photo.

- ✔ **Stacked pictures:** This one reveals the "macro" presets shown in the figure on the left; I've applied the *20's Vintage* preset to the image.

- ✔ **Funnel (at least I think that's what it is):** This icon reveals tools for sharpening your photo, turning it into a pencil sketch (shown in the figure on the right), and applying effects such as B & W, sepia tone, night vision, and heat map.

- ✔ **Color wheel:** This icon reveals the serious image-editing controls you see in the figure on the right below: exposure, contrast, highlights, shadows, saturation, color temperature, levels, and RGB. I love the Photoshop-like histogram for adjusting relative brightness levels, as shown in the figure on the right.

- ✔ **Line chart:** This one gives you a Photoshop-like Levels curve tool for precise color correction.

- ✔ **Eyeball:** An easy-to-use red-eye-removal tool.

- ✔ **Star:** This icon enables you to drag a variety of cartoon balloons and shapes onto your photos, with complete control over the outline, fill, and text colors. You also have a choice of five fonts (but none look as much like a comic book as the exclusive font used by Comic Touch).

> ✔ **Square:** Tapping this icon (shown in the figure on the right) discloses the frames, backgrounds, and effects options. The tape on the corners of the image is one of the preset frame options; the blue background is one of the background color options; and the reflection below the picture is one of the special-effects options.

I tried a lot of programs with similar features and Photogene delivers the most bang for the buck (okay, four bucks). And, unlike most similar apps, it can edit high-resolution RAW files. If you use your iPad to retouch photos, you should definitely have this app in your arsenal.

Best features

All of Photogene's features are really quite excellent, so I think the best thing about this app is that it has so many high-quality image-editing tools. The intuitive and uncluttered user interface and unlimited undo/ redo support are not too shabby, either.

Worst features

My big complaint is that the shadow-effect options for frames are kind of ugly and there's no way to adjust their transparency.

My minor gripe is that the pencil, reflection, and frame effects work well and deliver beautiful results on most images, but I wish there were more special effects such as crayon, oil paint, mosaic, or watercolor. If those effects existed and looked as good as the pencil, reflection, and most of the frame effects, they'd be awesome!

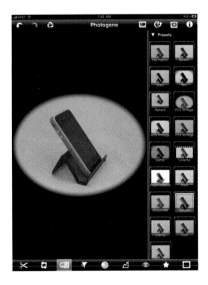
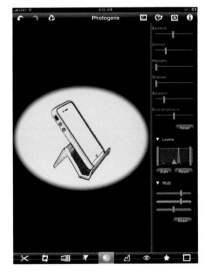

Strip Designer
$2.99

This app is fun and easy to use, and it provides numerous creative options for turning your photos into comic strips or graphic novels. And while I enjoy using it on my iPhone, the iPad version provides a much better user experience.

The first thing you do is select one of the many available page layout templates, as shown in the figure on the left below. Then you populate the panels by choosing photos from your Photos app library — or a map of any location in the world. Inserting a map or maps of your creation into a comic strip is a brilliant integration of iPad technologies.

Once you've selected a picture or map for a panel, you can modify it in various ways if you want. In the figure on the right below, for example, I'm applying the halftone filter to the picture of Allie and the dog (top left). You can apply any or all of the other effects — grayscale, sepia tone, invert, sketch, and so on — to any image or map in any panel of your comic.

But that's just the beginning. Now you can add embellishments like cartoon balloons, text blocks, shapes, stickers, borders, cutouts, and more. Cartoon balloons do more than just let you put words in someone's mouth. They also include arrows, stars, hearts, and ovals.

Then there are dozens of interesting stickers that let you make your strip even more comic-like. I used a couple — Ka-Boom and BAM — in the figure on the right.

I'm also pretty impressed with the Cutout feature, which lets you store an image or part of image — say, your logo or other "branding" — and reuse it in any panel or page with one tap.

Now, in addition to all the creative possibilities I've described so far, you also have the option of choosing a different page-layout template for any page at any time. Better still, you can preview your images in a number of different layouts very quickly and easily.

You can change page layout templates at any time, but here's a word to the wise: Do it *after* you add your photos or maps but *before* you add any text, bubbles, stamps, or other embellishments to your panels. And here's why: Some or all of the embellishments you place will appear in the wrong location in other page layouts. I'm just sayin'

you'll save yourself work if you try different page layouts *before* you embellish rather than after.

Finally, as you'd expect, Strip Designer has export and social-media options galore, making it easy to share your strips with others via e-mail (at normal or high resolution), Facebook, Flickr, and Twitter.

It adds up to easy-to-use tools for creating comic strips that look (at least in my humble opinion) extremely cool, as you can clearly see in the figure on the right.

Or not. But if you think my comic shows even an inkling of promise, you'll have a ball with Strip Designer.

Best features

Choices. This app is all about choices. Its myriad of page templates, filters, visual effects, cartoon balloons, stickers, and cutouts provide almost infinite creative options.

Worst features

Choosing a different page template can shift elements, which can cause extra work for you.

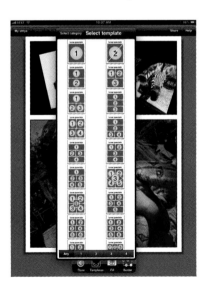

Adobe Photoshop Express
Free

Another excellent choice for improving photos, Adobe Photoshop Express has all the features you'd expect from an app that bears the Photoshop name — crop, rotate, flip, exposure, saturation, tint, and color-to-black-and-white conversions. I don't much care for some of the filters and special effects, such as Border and Rainbow, but I like almost everything else about the app.

Wondering why I recommend it? Well, I really like the way it's integrated with my Photoshop.com account. I can upload to and download from my online photo library and use the more advanced Photoshop.com image-editing tools for images that need more help than even Photogene can provide.

ArtStudio
$4.99

I picked this excellent, pro-quality painting-and-drawing program because many people think it's every bit as useful for professional illustration as the aforementioned Brushes. I'm not an artist by any stretch of the imagination, but I'd have a hard time choosing one over the other. In this case, they're both excellent.

But ArtStudio has one more thing Brushes does not: Art Lessons. Though I'm still not an artist, I did learn to draw a passable dog and cat. Kinda sorta. The lessons show you how to create a 3D drawing, and how to draw animals, faces, and humans. They're even kind of fun as you trace over every stroke in each lesson.

The Guardian Eyewitness
Free

It's brought to you by Canon but they're not all in your face about it (a discreet little logo that's not that bad). The app showcases "the world's most distinctive and provocative photographs." It's just a fancy photo gallery but the photos are generally superb. And the Pro Tips that accompany them — such as "very fast shutter speed" and "shallow depth of field" — are useful if you are the type of photographer who likes to know how to "do stuff" to make your pictures more interesting or dramatic.

Even if you hate photography, check it out for the pictures, which are often spectacular.

Reel Director
$3.99

Reel Director is an amazing app that lets you do great things with video files. It's hard to believe, but Reel Director lets you combine and rearrange clips, add text overlays, add really cool opening and closing credits and title cards, and — my favorite feature — includes 28 really sweet transitions, which have animated previews and can be applied globally to an entire project.

Reel Director isn't Final Cut Pro or even iMovie, but it does let you do amazing things with video using nothing but your iPad. And since it's a hybrid app, you can use the same $3.99 app on your iPhone or iPod touch.

TiltShift Generator for iPad — Fake DSLR
$2.99

This one's another one-trick pony but that trick is pretty slick . . . . This app creates dramatic depth-of-field effects that look almost as good as that amazing depth of field you can only really capture with an expensive Digital SLR camera and a decent lens.

To give your photo depth of field, you tap the spot you want in focus. In a few seconds, your picture magically appears is if it had been shot with a very shallow depth of field. Using a great set of interactive slider controls, you can adjust the depth-of-field effect in near-real time.

Used judiciously, this app can turn a pretty good photo shot with a cheap camera (or a phone) into a stunning shot.

2 Book-Related Apps

Audiobook Player HD
$0.99

My wife and I have always enjoyed listening to audiobooks in our cars. First we listened to cassette tapes; then we listened to CDs; and now we use our iPads (and iPhones). Until recently, we spent $10 to $20 each month on audiobooks from Audible.com (www.audible.com). Then we discovered the fantastic Audiobook Player HD app from Alex Sokirynsky. With Audiobook Player HD, we can easily find, download, and listen to thousands of free audio books.

I liked the iPhone version of this app so much that I included it in *Incredible iPhone Apps For Dummies*. And today, the iTunes App Store description of Audiobook Player for the iPhone/iPod touch quotes yours truly saying it is the "easiest way to find and download free audiobooks."

That's only half of the story. I went on to explain that it offers several ways to browse or search for titles that interest you, as you can see in the figure on the left below.

I'd be remiss, gentle reader, if I didn't at least mention that Audiobook Player HD gets almost all of its content from Librivox (http://librivox.org), a non-commercial, non-profit, ad-free project run by volunteers. Librivox donates all of its volunteer-made recordings to the public domain.

If you don't want to pay 99¢ or you don't care for this app, you can visit the Librivox Web site, download all the audiobooks you like, and import them into iTunes. Audiobook Player HD just makes it easier to find and manage your audiobook library because it lets you download new audiobook titles right to your iPad and listen to them immediately. And Audiobook Player HD even breaks the files into chapters.

Best features

One of the best things about Audiobook Player HD is that (unlike the audiobooks you purchase from Audible.com) you can download free audiobooks one chapter at a time, as shown in the figure on the right, which helps you conserve storage space on your iPad.

Another nice feature of Audiobook Player HD is that you can download new titles or chapters over Wi-Fi or 3G (if your iPad is equipped with 3G, of course).

Worst features

Although the 2,300 free books include classics in the public domain, such as *The Adventures of Tom Sawyer, Aesop's Fables, Beyond Good and Evil, The Count of Monte Cristo, The Curious Case of Benjamin Button, Pride and Prejudice, Robinson Crusoe,* and *A Tale of Two Cities,* there are few (if any) audiobooks written during *our* lifetimes. This isn't the app's fault, but I still consider it a shortcoming.

If you're looking for current bestsellers or more contemporary fare, the iTunes Store's Audiobook section has a pretty good selection. Keep in mind that the same audiobook you find in the iTunes store often costs less at `www.audible.com`. You might also check out the AudibleListener Gold plan. My wife and I pay just $14.95 per month to download one audiobook a month, even if the audiobook's list price is substantially higher (as most of them are).

Comics
Free

The Comics app is a front-end to the largest comic-book library online, offers a ton of free content, and provides a well-designed interface that makes viewing comics on a small screen more pleasant than other comic-book reader apps.

Comics is actually three different apps rolled into one. First and foremost, it's a fantastic way of reading comic books on a 3.5-inch touchscreen. It's also a comic-book store — with hundreds of individual comics from dozens of different publishers, including big guns like Marvel and DC Comics, as well as more cutting-edge providers such as Arcana Comics, Devil's Due, Digital Webbing, Red 5, Zenescope, and many others. Last but not least, it's a great way to organize the comics you own on your iPad so you can find the one you want quickly and easily.

Let's start with the viewer. Wired.com says Comics "solves the problem of reading comics on the small screen," and I agree. The comics are presented in Comixology's patented Guided View, which keeps the page intact as its creators intended. It "guides" you from panel to panel with beautiful transition animations, panning across frames and offering dramatic pull-backs that enhance the viewing experience, as shown in the figure on the left (which is from Amazing Spider-Man #1, an original copy of which might cost you up to $75,000 at auction but is available for just $1.99 in the Comics app's built-in comic-book store).

In all fairness, comic-book purists like my friend Andy Ihnatko don't much care for enhancements such as Guided View. In fact, he recently wrote an article for the *Chicago Sun-Times* in which he expressed his distain for such frippery: "Even when 'motion comics' are done with great expense and care (such as Marvel's recent 'Spider-Woman' offering) the overall effect is sock-puppety at best."

Some people say opinions are like noses (or other body parts not normally mentioned in a G-rated book such as this) because everybody has one. I'm sorry, Andy, but in my humble opinion, the animations are innovative and not at all "sock-puppety." In fact, I think Comixology's Guided View looks much better than the other comic-book reader apps that abruptly jump from panel to panel. Call me ignorant or unsophisticated or whatever you like, but I say Guided View is very cool and is a reason to love this app.

The free Comics app lets you download dozens of free comics when you first launch it, and more freebies are added each and every week.

To find comics — free or paid — just use the Comics app's excellent in-app comic store (see the figure on the right), which offers thousands of comics and series and generally lets you download the first issue in a series for free to see if you like it enough to buy subsequent issues. Most of the comics in the store cost between 99¢ and $1.99.

New releases are available every Wednesday, so visit the store often to check out the latest and greatest offerings. And by the way, Comics offers push notifications so you'll never miss a new issue of your favorite comic-book series.

Finally, both the store and your personal comic collection are well organized and easy to use.

Best features

Comics provides a fantastic viewing experience — immersive, enjoyable, and more cinematic than you expect from a comic book.

Worst features

Comics offers lots of different comics, but I've never heard of many of them. Although that's not necessarily a bad thing, I'd love to be able to buy more issues of vintage comics from Marvel and DC Comics, such as *Spider-Man*, *Batman*, *Superman*, *Fantastic Four*, and *Iron Man*.

Green Eggs and Ham
$3.99

That Sam-I-Am
That Sam-I-Am
I do not like
that Sam-I-Am

—Dr. Seuss

I remember reading the Dr. Seuss stories to my kids (now grown) years ago. And while I'm reluctant to recommend an app that reads Seuss to your kids for you, this app (actually apps) is so darn cute and so nicely done that I can't help myself. By all means read to your kids. But for those times when you just *can't* read to your kiddos, any of the Dr. Seuss iPad apps is the next best thing.

You see, while I've chosen to include *Green Eggs and Ham* in this chapter, it is but one of more than a dozen Dr, Seuss books that have been lovingly translated into iPad apps by Oceanhouse Media. Each of the book/apps, which include *The Cat in the Hat, How the Grinch Stole Christmas, Hop on Pop, The Lorax, Dr. Seuss's ABCs,* and *One Fish, Two Fish, Red Fish, Blue Fish*, to name just a few, is a complete Dr. Seuss book with all the words and illustrations you remember from your kids' childhood (or even your own childhood). Each story is presented with animation, audio, interactivity, plus, of course, lots of whimsical humor and that trademark Seussian wordplay.

All of the Seuss book/apps offer three modes of play:

- ✔ **Read to Me:** Each page is read aloud. When you're ready for the next page, you swipe a finger from right to left anywhere on screen.

- ✔ **Read It Myself:** The text isn't read aloud; swipe a finger to change the page.

- ✔ **Auto Play:** Automatically reads the entire story aloud, advancing from page to page without any tapping or swiping.

In all three modes the story is shown one page at a time and you can tap any word in the text (such as "boat" in the image below) to hear it pronounced. Or, if you press and hold anywhere in a block of text, the entire block is read aloud. And you can tap any item on the screen at any time to see its name (as shown for Tree, Support, Flag, and Boat in the image below) and hear its pronunciation (not shown or heard below).

The narration is quite professional and the sound effects are cute and clever. Tap a mouse and it squeaks. Tap a machine and it thrums. Tap a car and it vrooms. And your kid will learn a little spelling and pronunciation every time he or she taps an object or word on the screen.

Disney Publishing offers a number of similar apps it calls "Read Alongs" (such as Toy Story Read Along and The Princess and the Frog Read Along). They're clever and have additional features like games, finger-painting, and sing-alongs. But they're also more than twice the price ($8.99 each). On the other hand, if your kids like the Dr. Seuss stories, they'll probably like the Disney offerings too.

I read this book to my kids when they were young; I recall how the words and pictures made us smile. The medium (a tablet device) is new, but the beloved artwork and words haven't changed.

Best features

These titles are totally faithful electronic translations of your favorite Dr. Seuss classics. The narration, interactivity, and sound effects will amuse your kids for hours and help develop their reading skills.

Worst features

The sound effects and narration do get a bit repetitive. For example, every time you tap Sam-I-Am, the same exact voice says his name the same exact way; some variety would be nice. Your kid may not mind but it got on my nerves after a while.

Kindle
Free

Amazon.com's free Kindle app lets you shop for hundreds of thousands of eBooks, newspapers, and magazines at Amazon.com and read them at your leisure on your iPad.

Before I tell you about the Kindle app, though, you need to know about the Kindle devices that it emulates.

The Kindle is Amazon.com's $139–$359 wireless handheld reading devices (the $189 Kindle is shown in the figure on the left), which lets you shop for, buy, and read Kindle books, magazines, and newspapers on its black-and-white screen.

Think of Kindle devices as a kind of one-trick black-and-white iPad.

The Kindle app for the iPad (see the figure on the right) does more or less the same things as a Kindle, but on your iPad's glorious color touchscreen. Amazon's Kindle store offers more than 350,000 books, as well as newspapers and magazines at prices well below their printed counterparts. You can read the books, newspapers, and magazines you buy on the Kindle device or on your iPad with the free Kindle app.

The best thing about reading anything on either a Kindle device or an iPad with the Kindle app is that the electronic versions of books almost always cost you a lot less than the printed versions. For example, some of the best deals are on *The New York Times* Best Sellers, which generally cost just $9.99 for the Kindle version. At press time, examples of best-selling titles include Lee Child's *61 hours* ($28.00 in print; 67% saved); James Patterson's *The 9th Judgment* ($27.99 in print; 64% saved); Randy Pausch's *The Last Lecture* ($21.95 in print; 54% saved); and Timothy Ferriss' *The 4-Hour Workweek* ($22.00 in print; 55% saved). Magazines and newspaper subscriptions are less expensive than their hard-copy counterparts, too. For example, *The New York Times* Kindle Edition costs $19.99 per month (versus up to $60 per month, depending on where you live), and many magazines are less than $2 per month.

How does the free Kindle iPad app stack up to the $189 Kindle? Glad you asked! The Kindle has a smaller black and white screen than your iPad (6-inches vs. 9.7-inches) and includes a physical keyboard. But it doesn't include e-mail, maps, a music player, or a video player, and, of course, you can't install the tens of thousands of cool iPad apps on it.

The Kindle iPad app lets you read in portrait or landscape mode, choose the text size, choose background and text colors, add bookmarks and highlights, and zoom in and out at will. You can also create notes that are backed up automatically, as well as synchronized with your Kindle device (if you happen to own one in addition to owning the Kindle iPad app). To be perfectly fair, the Kindle iPad app lacks some of the Kindle device's features, such as a battery that lasts for days, text-to-speech, and full-text search. That said, do you really want to pay more than $100 or more to lug around a device just to read books and newspapers on a black-and-white screen? I thought not.

On the other hand, the Amazon Kindle bookstore has way, way more books (at least at this writing) than does the Apple iBooks bookstore. So this free app offers you access to a huge number of books, magazines, and newspapers that may not be available in the iBooks store.

Best features

The best thing about the Kindle app is that the Kindle store has a huge selection of titles, and you can carry almost anything you care to read in your pocket without spending $189 on a separate electronic device.

Worst features

You can't buy books from within the app, and after using iBooks (covered later in this chapter) it feels kind of awkward to shop for and purchase books using a Web browser. And, as I mentioned earlier, the iPad app lacks a search function and text-to-speech.

Stanza

Free

Stanza is another free eBook reader with more and better features than the Kindle app but a significantly smaller selection of titles.

Unlike the Kindle, Stanza doesn't offer a $189 handheld device, but I suspect you won't care.

Stanza has all the features that are missing from the Kindle app and more. Some of Stanza's niceties include almost infinite control over page layout, so you can specify not only font size but also margins, line and paragraph spacing, indentation, page color, and more, some of which are shown in the figure on the left below. Being able to adjust layout settings makes a huge difference, especially if you read in a variety of places with different types of lighting.

You can look up words using the built-in dictionary and jot down annotations. Plus, you can search for a word or phrase in any book, sort your library by title or author, or even create custom collections within your library. And, although this is kind of silly, if you don't like the cover that came with a book, you can replace it with other artwork using Stanza's Cover Lookup feature.

You can set multiple bookmarks in each book, and if you leave the app for any reason (a phone call, text message, or just because your eyes are tired) Stanza remembers where you left off and takes you back to that page the next time you launch the app.

If you read in multiple languages, you'll be pleased to know that the Stanza app includes built-in support for English, French, German, Italian, Spanish, Chinese, Japanese, Russian, Danish, Portuguese, and Swedish.

Best of all, Stanza has a set of fabulous built-in catalogs (some of which are shown in the figure on the right below), so you can find and download free content and purchase contemporary books without leaving the app, which is something you can't do with the Kindle app.

With the Kindle, you're limited to content you get at the Kindle Store on Amazon.com. Stanza offers titles from multiple sources, including Random House Free Library, Harlequin Books, and all 25,000+ books from Project Gutenberg.

Some of the available authors include Stephanie Meyer (*Twilight*), Dan Brown (*The DaVinci Code*), Malcom Gladwell, (*Blink*), Barack Obama

(*The Audacity of Hope*), Stephen King (too many titles to name), and James Patterson (ditto).

Stanza offers access to a lot of free books, probably more than any other app I've tested, including most (if not all) of the titles found in Free Books and Wattpad, as well as other titles from authors such as Edgar Allan Poe, Oscar Wilde, Sir Arthur Conan Doyle, and P. G. Wodehouse.

The Stanza catalogs are easy to use and they make finding titles a breeze. Most catalogs let you browse by author, title, or subject; some offer additional options such as "bookshelves, popular titles, and recent releases." Or you can use Stanza's excellent search mechanism to find what you're looking for across all Stanza catalogs.

This app has been lauded by *TIME* magazine (Top 11 iPad Apps), *PC Magazine* (Editor's Choice), *Wired* (10 Most Awesome iPad Apps), and BestAppEver.com. Because Stanza is free, you have no excuse not to give it a try.

Best features

I love having complete control over the way my pages look. I wish every app I use to read anything had this feature. I also like all the thoughtful touches such as search, built-in dictionary, and instant annotation.

Worst features

The biggest drawback to this app is its smaller selection of current titles (compared to Kindle).

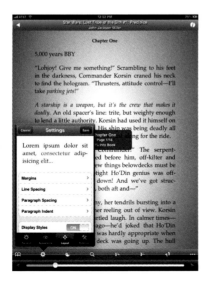
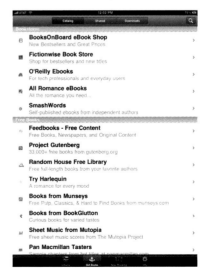

Free Books — 23,469 classics to go
Free

The name says it all . . . this app lets you download and read 23,469 classic books. There are other apps that offer similar content but if you're looking for a free app that does nothing but offer you free reading material — novels, autobiographies, letters, plays, poems, and more — look no further.

With its well-organized collections of various types of literature (Myths, Horror, Satire, Short Stories, Spy Stories, Thrillers, and such), Free Books makes it easy to find something good to read, easy to download what you've found to your iPad, and easy to enjoy reading it on Free Books' simple, uncluttered interface.

iBooks
Free

Just as your iPad's App Store and iTunes apps let you browse, search for, and purchase apps and music using your iPad, iBooks lets you use your iPad to browse, search for, and purchase books from Apple's iBookstore. Book pricing is similar to that of Kindle books, but the iBooks selection is much smaller. That said, iBooks is one of my favorite apps for reading text on my iPad screen, with easy and convenient management of screen brightness, font size, and typeface. It has a comprehensive search feature, highlighting, and note-taking — and it can read PDF documents as well as iBooks.

It's free, so you've got nothing to lose by checking it out.

Self-Help Classics
$0.99 US

They say that if something sounds too good to be true, it usually is. With the complete text of 16 self-help books for less than a buck, Self-Help Classics isn't one of those things. It's good *and* it's true.

The titles include *Think and Grow Rich* by Napoleon Hill, *The Master Key System* by Charles F. Haanel, *The Art of Public Speaking* by Dale Carnegie and Joseph Berg Esenwein, plus the autobiography of Andrew Carnegie, America's first self-proclaimed billionaire.

Then there's the app itself, which is nicely designed and has bookmarks, font-size control, navigation shortcut buttons, and (yea!) AutoScroll. Furthermore, the text is nicely set and easy to read.

Shakespeare
Free

If you're a fan of the Bard, you'll love this free app, which includes the full texts of 40 plays, all 6 poems, all 154 sonnets, and a searchable concordance.

Produced in part by PlayShakespeare.com, which is known as "the ultimate free Shakespeare resource," the works in this app are drawn from the First Folio of 1623 (and the Quartos where applicable) as well as the Globe Edition of 1866, re-edited and updated to reflect the editorial standards of PlayShakespeare.com's scholarly team.

Finally, if you really like Shakespeare, you can upgrade to the "Pro" version, which adds portraits, a glossary, quotes, facts, and scansion, for $9.99.

Wattpad
Free

Wattpad promotes itself as the world's most popular e-book community and a place for readers and writers to discover, share, and connect. That's an apt description that pretty much sums up what makes Wattpad so different from the other apps in this chapter. Where other apps feature previously published works, Wattpad is all about the unpublished works of fledgling authors.

The interface for searching and browsing is well designed, making it easy to find something interesting to read among the 100,000 available (and free) titles. Then you can cast votes, provide feedback, share with friends, and/or become a fan.

It's not all good, but I think you'll be surprised at how good many of the titles actually are.

3 Business

 ## iAnnotate PDF
$9.99

PDFs have become a mainstay of many business communications, and the iPad makes a great PDF reader. But some people need to make actual notes on their PDF files. Now, I realize that if you're among those who already annotate their PDFs, you already know this — but for everyone else, I'm talking about making notes, highlighting, drawing boxes . . . . You know, annotating.

There are six basic ways you can annotate with this app: You can add a comment that lives in its own box with the Note feature; you can use the Pencil tool to doodle, scribble, or write; you can make Straight Lines with the ruler icon, make Highlights (with more colors than you can shake a stick at), or Underscore and Strikeout text. In the figure below, you'll see examples of several of those methods.

 You can use iAnnotate's Pencil tool and a Pogo Stylus from Ten One Design (Bob says he prefers Styli from http://beststylus.com) to make handwritten notes to your heart's content!

Using these tools is all very straightforward: Tap the Note tool and then tap where you want to drop your note. Up comes a box for you to type in, along with the iPad's keyboard. Tap the Pencil and start doodling or writing. Tap the ruler for a Straight Line and then tap and drag within your document, wherever you want the line to go. Highlighting works just the way you think it should: Just tap the tool, then tap and drag to highlight the text or images you want to highlight. The same goes with the Underscore and Strikeout tools.

When you're done, tap the X icon in the upper-right corner of your screen to close that particular tool.

 If you want to erase (or edit!) one of your annotations, tap it and a bar comes up with several tools relating to your annotation. Tap the X to get a Delete option, tap the "-" icon to collapse the bar. Tap the little pencil icon to add a note (for instance, "I highlighted this because . . . "), or the pin icon to pin the editing bar in place.

You might be asking yourself, *Hey, how do I even get these PDFs onto my iPad?* There are several ways to do so:

- ✔ Send PDFs from your e-mail to iAnnotate by using the "Open With" command in those apps.

- ✔ Use the integrated browser to download PDFs from a Web page.

- ✔ Transfer files using iTunes.

- ✔ Use a companion app for Mac and Windows called Aji PDF Service that lets you browse a folder on your desktop computer.

- ✔ Use Dropbox, one of my favorite iPad apps/services, to download and upload files from all your computers and iOS devices (this is definitely my favorite way to bring PDFs onto my iPad).

 One of the best things about iAnnotate is the fantastic built-in help system that includes interactive help and provides overlays with explanations.

Best features

It's easy to use, has a great interface, and it integrates with Dropbox.

Worst features

I'd like to see some built-in shapes such as boxes and circles I can use for my notes, but that's a very small quibble.

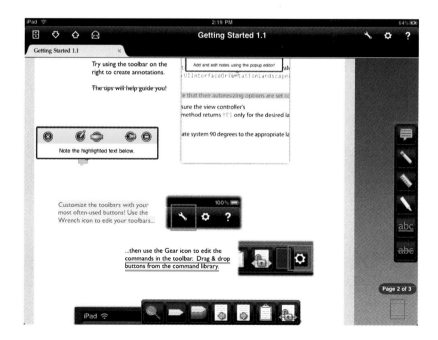

OmniGraffle
$49.99

If I had to pick just one company (outside of Apple) that I thought really grokked the iPad, it would have to be The Omni Group. These people really seem to have that whole touch-interface thing in their DNA. This whole book is full of great iPad apps, but The Omni Group's offerings definitely stand out among the standouts.

OmniGraffle has long been a Mac staple for people who need to make flowcharts, diagrams, and other layout ideas and designs. When the company brought this program to the iPad, they rethought it from the ground up. In fact, they told me that although the Mac version has been around for a long time, some things they learned on the iPad will go into the desktop version (it's usually vice versa). The key to this app is simply to embrace tapping, dragging, and multi-touch gestures for creating and editing your projects. In the figure below you'll see a bar with the project's name in the middle. On the left is a Documents button, your Undo button, and a little box-like icon for selecting groups of elements for group editing. You can also control how many canvases and layers you use.

Another way to select multiple items for group edits is to tap once on your first element, and then keep your finger on the screen while you tap other elements. I just tried it and it worked!

On the right is an "i" button that gives you details and options for whatever is selected, a square icon for choosing what kind of element to add, and a pencil icon for freehand-drawing squares or freeform shapes. To place an element from its palette, just drag it where you want it. To place a text label, double-tap where you want it to be and the keyboard interface comes up. To edit an existing element, tap it to select it for resizing or tap, hold, and release for a contextual editing menu. To reuse a particular element, tap, hold, and release on that element and choose Copy in the contextual menu. Then just tap, hold, and release somewhere else; choose Paste if you want to duplicate your element. The rest is pinching and zooming to resize elements or to zoom in on your canvas.

One of the nice features of this app is that it can keep the lines in place that connect two elements, even when you move one. Say you're making a flowchart like the one in the figure below. I haven't made a flowchart in a long time, and I had to figure out how to chart my (astonishingly bad) workflow for writing this book. I had to move things around quite a bit, but my arrows stayed connected, even while I rearranged my circles and squares and things.

TIP

If you want your flowcharts and diagrams to be lined up and even, dynamic guidelines appear when you're adjusting the size and position of elements next to one another.

You can make more complex diagrams and flowcharts than my (hopefully amusing) effort below. One of the sample charts, for instance, shows the major parts of a commercial espresso machine — complex shapes, shading, dials, knobs, and such, all drawn with OmniGraffle.

Now, if $49.99 is too much for you to spend, try Whiteboard HD ($5.99), or Instaviz ($9.99) for less expensive options.

Best features

I love how intuitive this app is — no instructions needed to start using it.

Worst features

There's no Redo feature — a strange omission for a company like The Omni Group — and many will find this app expensive.

Note from Bob: This app appears in Chapter 11 (Productivity) as well as in this chapter — it fits easily in either category, and we both love it.

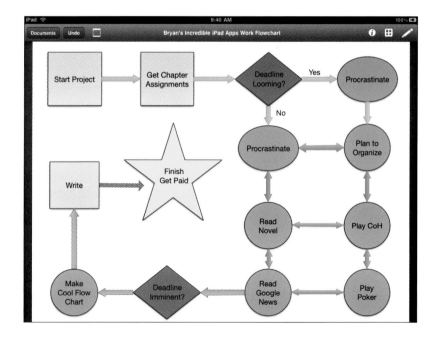

Pages
$9.99

I tell you what, Pages is the bee's knees. I listened to Apple execs tell us that the iPad would fulfill most people's computing needs in the future, and I quietly doubted just how soon that would happen until I got my hands on this app.

If you're new to the world of Apple-designed software, Pages is the company's word-processing software for Mac (and now iPad). It can't do everything Word does — it's aimed much more at consumers than Word is — but everything it *does* do it does extremely well. Letters, résumés, thank-you notes and cards, newsletters, proposals, reports, term papers, even posters and flyers . . . these are the kinds of things that Pages does well, and it makes doing them on the iPad pretty darned easy.

The key to this competence is the effort Apple put into reworking the user interface. They didn't try to shoehorn a desktop app into the iPad; they built the app from the ground up to be a word processor with a touch interface. This was one of the first iPad apps released, and I think Apple really wanted to show other developers what could be done. The result is that (thanks to some great use of gestures) you don't need a mouse. The app is *intended* to be used with pinches, zooms, swipes, and multifinger gestures, and I'm here to tell you that this is important for making it work well on the iPad.

The other key ingredient is that Apple made context king. The tools that are available on the screen depend entirely on what you're doing or have selected — and that keeps the app from becoming cluttered. When you're working on your document, the iPad's screen real estate is filled with that document, and not with a lot of tools and palettes you're not using.

At the top of the screen is a menu bar, as you can see in the figure below. You have a button for accessing your documents (or creating new ones), the Undo/Redo button, the title of the document you're working on, and some tools for manipulating text and objects. The "i" button has specific controls for manipulating whatever you've selected. If you're typing, it will have style, list, and layout options. If you select an image, it offers style options and ways to manipulate the image (such as flipping or aligning it). If you insert a chart, it gives you controls for the chart. It made instant sense to me on first use. The landscape button next to it allows you to add objects to your document. Photos in your library, tables, and shapes are all no more than a couple of taps away. The little wrench offers access to the in-app Help system and document-setup controls (margins, headers, footers, and such); the double-headed arrow gives you a full-screen view of your document.

One of the coolest things about Pages is the way objects work. Once you drop, say, a photo, you can move it, resize it, change the style, or even rotate it, and the text will just auto-flow around it in real time. It makes layout and design so easy to do that you may have to try it to truly appreciate it.

The app comes with 16 templates that make all the things I listed above even easier. You can share files via e-mail and with Apple's free iWork.com account. You can export a file as a Pages, Word, or PDF file. Whether you need to work on your files on the go or just want to use your iPad for some common tasks, Pages is an awesome app. I even typed up this review on my iPad with Pages.

Best features

Fantastic controls and a remarkably intuitive user interface make Pages a pleasure to work on.

Worst features

I wish Apple would add Dropbox support to its apps for some additional ways of moving files around.

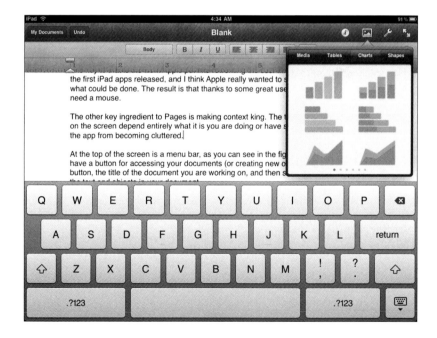

PrintCentral for iPad
$9.99

It seems strange that Apple hasn't made printing a core service in iOS that every app can tap into. Instead, we have a series of apps that bring the art of printing to the iPad and iPhone, each in its own different way. PrintCentral is the best of all those I tested.

News Flash: Apple just announced that printing services will be added to iOS 4.2, which is scheduled for release in November of 2010. Until then, PrintCentral is the best solution for printing from your iPad. Well, sort of — because it's really one of several different apps that the developer, EuroSmartz, has published under a series of different names; all do various combinations of the same thing. PrintCentral, Print n Share (which Bob selected for Chapter 11), NotePrinter, Printing for everyday . . . . Heck, even AltaMail is basically the same app. Still, the apps work, and PrintCentral works best, so let's look at it!

Launch PrintCental and you'll get a file browser. There's a Shared Files directory, a Clip Archive for items that have been copied to your clipboard, and a single file called Getting Started. If you tap on that file, you'll find instructions on how to make this printing thing work. As I noted above, Apple hasn't made this a core service in iOS, so it's harder to set up than it should be, but it's not *that* hard, so don't be intimidated!

There are two basic ways to use PrintCental. The first offers the best-quality printing, but it requires an intermediary print server (called WePrint) that you install on your Mac or PC. It's free from EuroSmartz, and it's easy to install and set up. In fact, most of the setup was automatic, with PrintCentral and WePrint finding each other easily. After I ran through some test printings, I could print from PrintCentral just fine. Plus, the app effectively serves as a document reader; you can read and edit several file formats directly within the app, manage your e-mail, and print from your e-mail in the process.

WePrint also allows you to designate a local shared folder on your computer for accessing files on your iPad. I was smart, and designated my Dropbox folder as my shared folder — killing a row of birds with one little rock! You can see the results of my handiwork in the figure below. It includes my local printing options in the foreground; in the background is a look at the special folder I set up in Dropbox for this screenshot, and part of the Business chapter for this very book. It's a Word file, and PrintCentral rendered it very well.

To access your shared folder, use the Places button at the bottom of your screen, as seen in the figure below.

PrintCentral can handle some printing without WePrint, but the best-quality options are available through the companion software. Also, WePrint can enable you to print over a 3G or EDGE connection, although the setup is cumbersome and not all networks and printers will allow this. The bottom line, though, is that if you want to print, you'll need an app like PrintCentral — at least until Apple does it right and adds printing services to iOS. Until that day, PrintCentral is your best choice.

If you were thinking about getting PrintCentral for both iPhone and iPad, get PrintBureau instead (if you search for "PrintBureau for all your printing needs," you'll go right to it). It's a Universal app that bundles both the iPhone and iPad PrintCentral apps together for $12.99.

Best features

I can print from my iPad, and it works!

Worst features

You have to get through an arcane interface to make this stuff work, but that's Apple's fault, in my opinion.

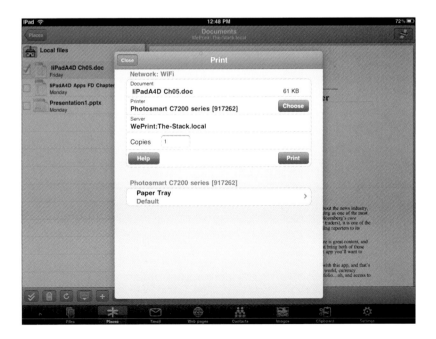

Quickoffice Connect Mobile Suite for iPad
$14.99 per year

As you read earlier, I'm a big fan of Apple's iWork apps for iPad, but there are other productivity suites available, too, like Quickoffice Connect Mobile Suite for iPad (which I just call Quickoffice from here on out!). I picked Quickoffice because it not only includes integrated Dropbox support for moving files back and forth on your iPad, it also supports Google Docs, Box.net, and MobileMe (both your MobileMe account and anyone else's iDisk Public Folder). And that's in addition to using iTunes to transfer files and Quickoffice Wi-Fi File Transfer, which you can do through a browser.

But really, get Dropbox if you haven't already! It's the best tool for moving and synching files between your Mac, PC, and iOS devices (heck, they support Android and BlackBerry, too!). It will make working with documents much easier for all your apps, whether or not they have built-in support for the service, thanks to the "Open With" feature in iOS.

So what does Quickoffice do? As the name suggests, it allows you to create and edit files in Microsoft Office formats. Not only can you can create, open, and edit Word documents using Quickword and crunch numbers in Excel spreadsheets using Quicksheets, you can also open and view — but not edit — PowerPoint files. (News flash: The developers say the editing capability will be added in an update.) Your editing tools are limited compared to what you get in desktop productivity suites for Mac and PC — especially the real Microsoft Office suite — but the basic formatting tools in this iPad app will be enough for the vast majority of on-the-go edits that most users are likely to want to make.

You can open Microsoft Office documents that are macro-enabled as read-only files, but you can't edit them. If you plan to edit your Office files on your iPad, be sure to use the common file formats (DOC, DOCX, TXT, XLS, XLT, and XLTX).

Check out the figure to the left below. Do you see those thumbnails on the right side of the screenshot? That's a really clever way of jumping from page to page in Quickoffice. Touch and hold the screen on the far edge of the right margin, and you get thumbnails of each page. The page that is highlighted in this thumbnail view has a page number on it, which is really handy if your document just has a lot of text on it (like the one I was using for my screenshot). Just slide your finger down the screen until you get the page you want. When you lift your finger, you go straight to that page. It's really nifty.

Another nice feature is the Multi-Edit Toolbox, which allows you to make several changes at one time to selected text (font, size, color, and paragraph formatting).

Undo is a tap away. In the figure to the left below, you'll see a sort of yin/yang symbol. Tap that and you get a pop-up menu for Undo and Redo. It's pretty simple.

The app's spreadsheet tool, Quicksheets, is pretty full-featured. You can edit the formatting and style of all of your cells, and it's easy to add new rows and columns. Editing a formula is straightforward (if you understand Excel formulas to begin with). In the figure to the right below, I took a perfectly fine formula and put some additional math at the end. It worked just fine, though I think I probably made accountants everywhere a little tense. Be that as it may, if you're comfortable in Excel, I think you'll be quite happy editing spreadsheets in Quicksheets. I'm hoping that Microsoft eventually brings us their own iPad Office apps, but until then Quickoffice is a good way to work with files on the go.

Best features

The thumbnail page-navigation implementation is a clever way to get through long documents, and I just love all the file-transfer services this app supports.

Worst features

This app would be even more compelling with some advanced editing tools. It definitely needs spell-check, too.

FileMaker Go for iPad
Free (or $9.99 for the Pro version)

FileMaker Go for iPad isn't a replacement database app for the desktop version of FileMaker Pro, but it's a great companion app for editing existing databases on the go. The app can connect directly to databases hosted on FileMaker Server or FileMaker Pro, and changes made to those databases happen live. But FileMaker Go also allows you to copy a database to your iPad for offline viewing and manipulation. The interface is great, and most FileMaker Pro features are supported, making this a must-have app for FileMaker Pro users.

FileMaker Go doesn't support file-synching, but you can copy files back to your hosted solution when you have an Internet connection.

Keynote
$9.99

As the second leg of Apple's iWork productivity suite, Keynote allows you to make presentations directly on your iPad. It offers text formatting and image manipulation, professional-looking templates, transitions, and great controls that make working with this app easy, fast, and fun. Many of Keynote's conventions mirror those in Pages, and if you're comfy in one (or all three, counting Numbers), you'll be pretty comfy in the others. Even if you're brand new to making presentations and you're leery of this touchscreen thing, you'll still make a better-looking presentation with Keynote on the iPad than anyone ever has with PowerPoint on a PC.

Numbers
$9.99

Numbers is Apple's spreadsheet app for its iWork suite, but I've never thought of it as a direct competitor to Microsoft Excel. Instead, it's more of a home-and-small-business spreadsheet app with an emphasis on turning data into great-looking graphs and charts. Numbers on iPad takes that a little farther by adding some viewing features that make the app good for using completed spreadsheets to get more data. As with Pages and Keynote, Apple has redesigned the interface with the touchscreen in mind, and it's remarkably easy to do things like tie a graph to a spreadsheet and manipulate the fields until you have what you need.

OmniGraphSketcher
$14.99

Hey look, here's another entry from The Omni Group. Yep, they're that good. OmniGraphSketcher is a dedicated app for making charts and graphs on the iPad (without spreadsheets). As with OmniGraffle, I found the controls and tools for this app to be extraordinarily intuitive, and I'm not even much of a charts-and-graphs kind of guy to begin with. Colors, grids, shapes, bars, points, circles and arrows . . . it's all here and easy to use. You can export your work through e-mail or drop it to your photo library for inclusion in another productivity tool. If you need to make professional-looking charts and graphs, you should start (and stop) with this app.

Prompster
$9.99

There are several teleprompter apps for the iPad. A couple of them are really good, but I picked Prompster to highlight because it includes an audio recorder right in the app so you can record your presentation as you give it. The basic idea is to use your iPad's wonderful display as a portable teleprompter. Import your text from e-mail or through iTunes, or type it up (or edit it) right there on your iPad. Set the scrolling speed and the size of your text, and you're off! Onscreen controls let you see the elapsed time, stop as needed, or adjust the speed and text size on the fly.

4 Entertainment

Acrobots
$0.99 US

The application description in the iTunes App Store for Acrobots says it's a "mesmerizing, physics-based toy," and I'll be darned if I can think of a more accurate description.

The so-called acrobots (or "bots" for short) are multicolored, gelatinous, acrobatic creatures with circular bodies and three slender arms that have suction cups at the ends (see the image on the left). The bots tumble, disconnect, reconnect, push off one another (and the edges of the screen), and float around in a smooth, colorful ballet.

By tilting or shaking your iPad, you can make the bots move on their own according to the settings you specify (as shown in the figure on the right). You can also tap any bot to flick it in any direction; the faster you flick, the faster the bot moves.

The five icons shown (from left to right) at the top of the screen in the images on the next page perform these tasks:

✔ **Plus sign:** Adds a bot.

✔ **Minus sign:** Removes a bot.

✔ **Light bulb:** Turns silhouette mode on and off. In silhouette mode, the bots turn a dark shade of blue and the background changes from black to light blue.

✔ **Target:** Opens the settings screen.

✔ **Question mark:** Displays the version number.

The settings screen, shown on the right, lets you control the physics that govern the bots' movement. You have complete control over the bots' size, balance, suction-cup stickiness, and movement speed, as well as the effects of gravity and air drag.

At the bottom of the screen are eight presets that control all six parameters at once. The setting I used in the figure on the right below is called Beasts; others include Teeter, Tumble, Spazz.

Here's a nice touch: If you start playing music on the iPod app, then close the iPod app and open Acrobots, you'll have a nice soundtrack for your bots' shenanigans. Try flicking bots in time to a Ramones tune (most are a staggering 170 beats per minute) or something more sedate. Music adds a whole new dimension to Acrobots, so give it a try.

If you're having trouble imagining what bots look like in motion, check out the Web-based Flash simulation of Acrobots at `www.vectorpark.com/acrobots`. There you can add and remove bots, flick them, and adjust their speed. But because you can't tilt or shake your computer, nor can you control individual physics attributes of the bots, the simulation isn't nearly as cool as the iPad version. Despite these shortcomings, it's still a good demo of what bot movements look like. If you need to be convinced that this app is cool, give the demo a try.

Best features

Acrobots is mesmerizing, fascinating, and, at least in my humble opinion, soothing. I can waste an inordinate amount of time flinging them around, shaking my iPad to scramble them, and observing the effects different settings have on the way the bots move. The app is also great for showing people something "cool" on your iPad.

Worst features

The effect of Acrobots would be even more stunning if there were sounds associated with suction cups attaching to and detaching from other suction cups, but the app doesn't include audio. That said, you can play music with your iPod while you play with Acrobots, which doesn't have the same effect as app-specific audio would, but it's still interesting.

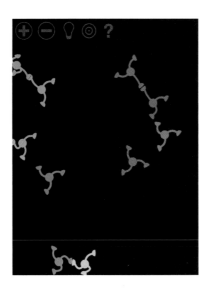

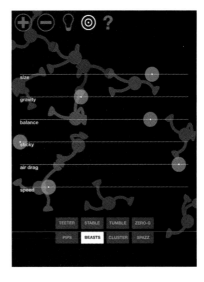

Bloom HD
$3.99 US

I think what I like best about Bloom HD is that it's uniquely difficult to describe. That's why I'm leaving the description to its co-creator, ambient music pioneer Brian Eno: "Bloom HD is an endless music machine, a music box for the 21st century. You can play it, and you can watch it play itself."

Okay. I realize that although that statement does capture the spirit of Bloom HD, it isn't particularly descriptive. So let me try to put it another way. To me, Bloom HD is one part musical instrument, one part ambient music generator, and one part music-derived art. In its interactive play mode, you tap your iPhone screen to create elaborate musical patterns and uniquely interesting melodies that are paired with colorful patterns of dots that appear when you tap the screen. For example, the figure on the left is what Bloom HD might look like after you've played it (by tapping) for a few minutes.

Each tap produces notes that sound to me like a 19th century music box mated with a Bösendorfer grand piano to produce a Fender Rhodes electric piano. The three join to sing in unison while random synthesized chord-like structures play softly in the background under the music box/piano tones. At times the chords sound like a string ensemble and at other times they sound like nothing else on earth. I mean that in the nicest way possible.

If you don't feel like tapping, you can let Bloom HD's generative music player take over to create an infinite selection of compositions with accompanying visuals.

Some might say that Bloom HD is the iPad equivalent of an infinite kaleidoscope with an ambient soundtrack created by Brian Eno. I'd say that's another apt description of Bloom HD.

When you play with Bloom HD, you can select the Classic, Infinite, or Freestyle modes. Each one offers a slightly different kind of audio and video experience. You can also choose to either Listen or Create. In Listen mode, Bloom HD produces the music for you, although you're free to add your own taps as well; in Create mode, Bloom HD leaves it to you to do the tapping.

Bloom HD has myriad settings you can tinker with to subtly alter what you see and hear, as you can see in the figure on the right. The app includes a dozen "moods" to choose from, which are preset combinations of colors and sounds, each with an interesting name such as Neroli, Ambrette, Labdanum, and Tolu.

Bloom HD is soothing to me, and I often play with it when I'm feeling stressed. If you're a fan of Brian Eno, into meditation, enjoy playing with apps that are soothing and relaxing, or if you just like playing with an interesting app, you'll appreciate Bloom HD as much as I do.

If you like Bloom HD, I urge you to check out Aphonium and Aphonium SE, which appear in Chapter 9 (the dedicated music chapter). And if you are wondering why Bloom is here in the Entertainment chapter and Aphonium is in the Music chapter, the answer is that Bloom actually did appear in the Music chapter of *Incredible iPhone Apps For Dummies*. But that was before Aphonium — which is even more musical instrument-like than Bloom — was released.

Best features

Bloom HD is totally unique; there's nothing else like it except, perhaps, the aforementioned Aphonium.

Worst features

It would be nice to have some additional sounds. The music box/Bösendorfer/Rhodes tones are beautiful, but variety is the spice of life. I'd love to hear some other sounds in Bloom HD.

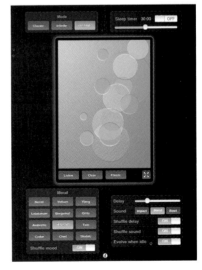

EWMust List   EW's Must List
Free

In a chapter about entertainment apps it seemed only right to include this app, which provides a glimpse of what's new in the world of popular entertainment. It's produced by *Entertainment Weekly* magazine, and it brings you ten new entertainment picks every Friday, as shown in the figure on the left below.

If that was the only thing this app had to offer, it might have still earned a spot in this chapter. But the app delivers much more — and presents everything in an appealing and easy-to-use format.

See the icons at the bottom of the figure on the left: *My Must List, Movies, TV, Music, Books,* and so on? Tap one and you'll see a dozen or more recent picks from that category.

For every item on every screen (each movie, book, CD, app, game, TV show, or other form of entertainment) there's a "details" screen like the one on the right below. This particular details screen is for Maroon 5's "Misery" video, and it has buttons that let you watch the music video, download the song or the Maroon 5 Essentials collection from the iTunes Store, or browse *Entertainment Weekly*'s Summer Songs gallery with a single tap of your finger. Other types of media may have different sets of options. For example, the details screen for the *Mad Men* TV show lets you download a free video or buy individual episodes from the iTunes Store, read *Entertainment Weekly*'s latest review of the show, or jump to the *Mad Men* hub on the *Entertainment Weekly* Web site. Screens for other media types may offer buttons that let you watch a trailer, download an app, subscribe to a related podcast, or visit a related Web site.

In other words, when you find an item that tickles your fancy, you'll be able to access more info on it with just a couple of taps.

It's all good stuff — but my favorite feature has to be My Must List. There's an Add to My Must List button for every item on every screen. Tap this button and the app saves the entire detail page on your Must List, which you can visit by tapping the My Must List button at the bottom of every screen. I like this because I often find a book, movie, CD, app, or TV show I'd like to know more about but don't have time to explore right then. Without My Must List I'd either forget the thing completely or waste a bunch of time trying to find it again. Which is to say My Must List acts as my long-term memory, which makes it a very good feature in my book.

If you're interested in popular culture, I can't think of a better way to keep up with what's new and interesting. While I don't have the time, patience, or interest to sit and read an entire issue of *Entertainment Weekly* from cover to cover, there are usually a couple of items each week that do interest me. This app makes it easy for me to peruse entertainment offerings that interest me without having to wade through a lot of stuff I don't care about. It really does offer me a snapshot of pop culture each week. This week, for example, the top ten includes two cable-TV programs, two books — one fiction, one nonfiction — two network TV programs, an Internet-only video, a video game, an offbeat theatrical movie release, and a DVD. Last week included a profile of a band and a box set by another artist.

It's kind of a guilty pleasure but very nicely done. If you're interested in what's popular today or what may be popular tomorrow, give it a try. You can't beat the price — it's free!

Best features

It's a quick and easy way to discover new movies, TV, music, books, games, apps, and other forms of popular media that interest you.

Worst features

It can take time to download new content, so you often have to wait a minute or two before the latest news appears on the screen.

EyeTV
$4.99* US

The EyeTV app provides three awesome TV-related features. With it I can

✔ Watch live TV in real time on my iPad wherever I have a 3G or Wi-Fi connection.

✔ Use my iPad to watch TV shows and movies I've recorded using EyeTV on my Mac, without having to synch them with or store them on my iPad.

✔ Remotely start recording live TV or schedule future recordings on my Mac at home.

Before you get too excited about EyeTV, know that there are a couple of provisos. See the asterisk next to the $4.99 price? It's there because to use this app you must have the EyeTV software and hardware running on your Mac at home. The EyeTV hardware and software packages, which let you watch and record television programming on your Mac screen, cost at least $119.95.

Having had the EyeTV hardware and software on my Mac for many years (long before the iPad was invented) I've felt it was worth every penny. Today I think that EyeTV hardware and software on my Mac plus the EyeTV iPad app may be the greatest combination since peanut butter and jelly. It's an awesome combo even at $124.94 ($119.95 + $4.99).

I love watching video on my iPad, especially when I'm stuck in a hotel room far from home or on an airplane that offers Wi-Fi service. Before the EyeTV app, I had to use iTunes to synch movies or TV shows that I might want to watch while I was on the road. Now I don't have to do that. Instead, I just fire up the EyeTV app on my iPad and choose from the hundreds of movies and TV shows I've recorded with the EyeTV device connected to my Mac.

Speaking of recording, the EyeTV app lets me start a recording at home or schedule one for the future. It includes a built-in program guide that shows me what's on now and for the next 10 days (figure on the left). If there's something I want to record (say the Season 2 opener of *Jersey Shore* on MTV as shown in the figure on the right below) I just tap the big blue Record button, and the EyeTV system on my Mac records the show so I can watch it on my iPad any time I like.

Perhaps the coolest feature of the EyeTV app is that I can watch live TV in real time anywhere there's Wi-Fi, as shown in the image on the left below. When I'm sitting at Starbucks enjoying a latte, I can watch the news live on any of my local TV channels, or watch CNN, MTV, VH1, or any of the other 70+ basic cable channels available on my EyeTV device back home.

One last thing: I'd be remiss if I didn't mention that if you're not interested in viewing live TV on your iPad or using an iPad app to schedule or start video recordings on your Mac — or if you're a Windows user — check out the Air Video app, which lets you stream pre-recorded video from your Mac or PC to your iPad, for only $2.99.

Best features

The best feature is using the EyeTV app on my iPad to schedule and record TV shows on my Mac and watch them at my convenience on my iPad. Though watching live TV on my iPad is pretty darn cool, too.

Worst features

First, the app requires you to also have an EyeTV hardware and software system ($119.95+). Second, EyeTV systems are Mac-only. And third, the app doesn't work nearly as well over 3G as it does over Wi-Fi.

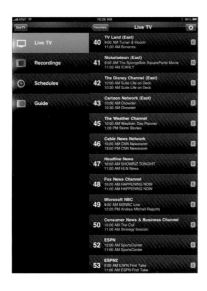

NPR for iPad
Free

The NPR app delivers some of the best programming that National Public Radio (aka NPR) has to offer — directly to your iPad. The app itself is elegant and easy to navigate, as befits a national institution like NPR. But unlike listening to your local NPR radio station, the NPR for iPad app lets you pick and choose what you want to hear (or read), as well as when you want to hear it.

If you like NPR programming, there's a lot to like about the NPR app, which offers a combination of news stories, hourly newscasts, music playlists, and specific NPR programs including all of my favorites — *Wait, Wait . . . Don't Tell Me, Car Talk, Fresh Air,* and *All Things Considered* — and many more. There's also a GPS-enabled Station Finder that can locate the closest NPR radio station so you can listen to NPR in real time.

In many ways, using the NPR app is superior to listening to your local NPR radio station. For one thing, everything in the app is available on demand. So I don't have to be near a radio at 10:00 a.m. on a Saturday to hear *Wait, Wait . . . Don't Tell Me* on my local NPR affiliate.

Another benefit is that many programs are broken into segments so you can listen to the parts that interest you and avoid the parts that don't. This is especially useful for shows that cover a variety of topics such as *Fresh Air* or *All Things Considered.* The image on the left below shows some of the segments from a recent *All Things Considered* program in the foreground and the app's Home screen in the background.

One cool feature I wish more apps would offer is the capability to select topics for offline reading. The figure on the right below shows my selection of Arts & Life topics in the foreground. Stories in any of those categories are downloaded automatically to my iPad so I can read them offline (that is, without an Internet connection) at my convenience. This is a very good feature indeed, especially if you spend much time on airplanes.

I also like that many stories provide you with a choice of text, audio, or both so you can read the story, listen to it, or do both (as you can see in the background of the figure on the right below).

Yet another thing I love about the NPR app is that I can tap the little plus sign for program segments or the Add All to Playlist button for entire programs to add the segment or program to my playlist. This makes it easy to save anything you want to see or hear but don't have the time to catch right now.

Other niceties include buttons that let you share a story, show, or segment with your friends via Twitter, Facebook, or even good old-fashioned e-mail. And if a program is available as a podcast in the iTunes Store — as *Car Talk, Wait, Wait . . . Don't Tell Me,* and *Fresh Air* are (to name a few) — there's a button that launches the iTunes Store app, where you can download individual episodes of that show. I listen to NPR a lot more these days than I ever thought I would and I think my wife listens to it even more. Wherever we go, the NPR app lets us enjoy our favorite NPR programming on demand. And the ability to choose which topics are downloaded and stored for offline reading is the icing on the cake.

Best features

The playlists are awesome, as is the capability to choose topics you want the app to download automatically for offline reading. The user interface is a delight to both the eyes and the ears. And you can't beat the price.

Worst features

I tried and tried to come up with something I dislike about this app but couldn't think of a single thing.

Air Video
$2.99

Do you have more movies than storage space on your iPad? Air Video solves the problem by making the video storage capacity of your devices limitless. (I say *devices* because the same app works on both iPads and iPhones.)

Just install the free Air Video Server app on your PC or Mac and specify the folder(s) to contain the video you want to watch on your device. That's all there is to it! And unlike iTunes, Air Video Server supports almost all video formats — and can convert most video on the fly, so there's no waiting to watch what you've chosen.

If your movie collection is bigger than your iPad's available storage space, you'll love Air Video.

IMDb Movies & TV
Free

IMDb stands for Internet Movie Database, which is probably the world's largest collection of information about movies, actors, directors, TV shows, and much more. Many an argument in my house was settled in mere seconds by searching for the actor, director, movie, TV show, or whatever triggered the dispute.

If that were all it did, it would be enough. But it also provides movie showtimes for local theatres, TV listings for your local time zone, recaps of yesterday's TV shows, movie trailers, reviews, and much more.

If you enjoy movies or TV, you should have this app on your iPad — absolutely, unequivocally, and without question.

Koi Pond HD/Koi Pond HD Lite
$1.99 US/Free

Picture a beautiful, crystal-clear pond with colorful koi swimming in its shallow water, with the soft sounds of nature in the background. Next, imagine sticking a finger in the water and watching the water ripple as the koi dart away.

Now picture what this scenario might be like on your iPad and you have Koi Pond HD. It comes with a variety of calming themes plus a pond editor to create your own watery wonderlands (paid version only).

Koi Pond HD is gorgeous, relaxing, and beautiful. What more could you ask from a $1.99 app?

 # Netflix
Free

The Netflix app lets you stream thousands of Netflix movies and TV shows to your iPad.

If you're not familiar with Netflix, it's a DVD-by-mail service that also lets you watch many of its TV shows and movies instantly on Netflix-ready devices such as a Mac, PC, Wii, PS3, Xbox 360, or iPad. There's a two-week free trial available at `www.netflix.com`; if you like it, memberships start at $8.99 a month.

If you're not a Netflix member, the service is definitely worth checking out. If you are already a Netflix member, download this app immediately (if you haven't already).

 # Uzu
$0.99

The iTunes Store description of Uzu begins, "Technically speaking, Uzu is a kinetic multitouch particle visualizer. Really it's a sort-of-math-physics-art-toy for anyone who ever loved spirographs, fireworks, planetariums, lava lamps, light sabers, pen lasers, Tesla coils, Christmas lights, or graphing calculators."

I don't know that I can explain it much better but I'll try: Touch the screen with any number of fingers from 1 to 10 and watch what happens to the multicolored dots and lines.

5 Finance

Bloomberg for iPad
Free (Ad-Supported) — Hybrid

Let me start this look at Bloomberg's iPad app by talking about the news industry, because the Bloomberg news organization is not only emerging as one of the most important financial news outlets on the planet (remember, Bloomberg's *core* business is providing financial data to Wall Street and other traders), it's also one of the few major news organizations of any type that has been *adding* reporters to its payroll in the last couple of years.

Why does that matter? Because there are great apps and there is great content, and Bloomberg for iPad is one of those terrific combinations that bring both of those benefits. If you want to follow finances on your iPad, this is an app you'll want to download.

Now that I've gushed a little bit, let's look at what you get with this app: Financial news, stock quotes, major indices from around the world, currency information, bond prices, the capability to track your stock portfolio . . . oh, and access to a lot of market-related podcasts.

Need more? Too bad, because you won't find it in one single app!

The home page of this app is divided up into five sections, as you'll see in the figure on the left below. You've got snapshot looks at Top News, Equity Indices, My Stocks, Currency, and then a block of large icons to access all of the app's major sections. Those icons are easy to read, but they take up a lot of space. Still, they make it easy to navigate the app.

Let's tap through to News page, which I think many users will use the most. There we get top stories divided into subsections of Worldwide, Most Read, Exclusive, Bonds, and Commodities. Some of those stories come with teaser graphics, but otherwise they include title, date, and how many minutes or hours old the story is. You can tap through on the title to read a story, or if you tap the section headers, you get taken to a page with additional stories that you can scroll through.

The My Stocks sections is the place for you to enter stocks you want to monitor; if you own those stocks, you can enter your position and purchase price to monitor their value in your portfolio. After you've done so, you get a nice snapshot view of those stocks. Tap through anywhere on a stock's display and you're taken to a detailed page — complete with a large graph of the stock's performance (with thumbnails to change the view to one day, one month, six months, and one year), as you can see in the figure on the right below.

If you've bought shares in a company at different times, you can add that stock more than once so you can keep track of the different positions and purchase prices of your holdings.

Best features

Great content, a great interface, timely news, podcasts . . . it's all great.

Worst features

I'd like the capability to customize the home page. The icons at the bottom are easy to read, but they're big, and I personally don't need all of them.

Daily Stocks
$19.99

I think that Daily Stocks is the kind of app that exemplifies the sort of specialized software that not only makes sense on the iPad, but is, in part, made possible *by* the iPad:

```
Screen Real Estate + Computing Power + App Store = Cool Specialization
```

Because of that, I'll risk getting a little out of my depth to talk about this rather cool app.

Unlike the plethora of stock-portfolio-tracking or financial-news-information apps, Daily Stocks provides the user with technical scans of the market (up to 91 such technical scans as of this writing). In other words, it's designed to highlight trends in the marketplace, using some highly technical analytical techniques (most of which are for fairly serious traders) so users can identify opportunities and risks.

The app works in landscape and portrait mode, but portrait mode shows you a little more information, so we'll focus on that. As you can see in the figure below, the left of the screen offers charts for the three major U.S. indices and five global indices.

It's the right two-thirds of the screen, however, that is dedicated to the real purpose of this app. At the top of the screen in the green bar are three tabs labeled JC (Japanese Candlesticks), OS (Overextended Stocks), and SS (Stock Scans). These are three different styles of reports, and each offers very different information.

In the trading world, a *candlestick* is a kind of bar graph. It shows the opening price of a stock and its closing price, with the color telling you whether it was a winning day (opening on the bottom, closing on the top) or a losing day (opening at the top, closing at the bottom). For Daily Stocks, a red candlestick represents a losing day and a green candlestick represents a winning day. Simple, eh? And more informative to traders than other graphs.

The JC tab offers ten Bullish trends, ten Bearish trends, and three Indecision trends. These are all attempts to understand where the market is headed, based on patterns identified in the past. In other words, the trend indicators are far from perfect (but their adherents tend to feel strongly about them). Those names you see, such as Falling Three Method or Engulfing, are all English approximations of the original Japanese names the patterns were given.

Trends with more information are shaded darker gray; a tap gives you a new screen that defines what the trend is supposed to identify and lists the stocks that match the pattern.

Overextended Stocks are stocks that have broken above their resistance levels (Overbought) or below their support levels (Oversold) or that have traveled beyond their Simple Moving Average (SMA). The OS tab gives you a list of the ten most Oversold or Overbought stocks compared to their SMAs over the last 9 to 200 days. You can tap through one of those ten stocks in any of the SMA views to get several graphs and charts.

Lastly, the Stock Scans tab gives you more than 50 reports of stocks that have met some specific criteria (New 52 Week High or Low, various volume levels, crossover reports, and many more).

These are all very technical kinds of reports and scans; if you're not an active trader, you probably don't need this app. If you are, however, you're likely to find it very useful.

Best features

This app offers an impressive number of reports and analysis scans.

Worst features

The app should be more customizable — and I'd like to be able to look up individual stocks to see whether they fit into any of the scans and reports offered by the app.

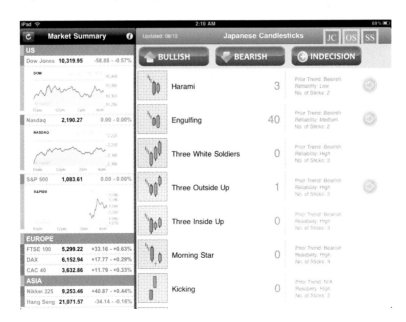

E*TRADE Mobile Pro for iPad
Free — Hybrid

Once upon a time, you needed a broker to buy and sell stocks — but today, if you have a computer with access to the Internet, you can effectively conduct your own stock transactions almost instantaneously. Or maybe instead of "today," that should be "before iOS devices," because now with E*TRADE Mobile Pro for iPad, you may even forget about your poor old computer and do all your trading with E*TRADE Mobile Pro.

With this app, you can buy and sell stocks and options, transfer money around on your E*TRADE accounts, set up or manage watch lists, monitor your orders, manage and receive alerts, monitor your portfolio, get stock quotes, and get news, all from within this very well-designed and elegant iPad app — and the company has done an excellent job of putting all that screen real estate to use.

E*TRADE has centered the interface on two rows of panels that each contain tools and reports you'll need to watch the markets, monitor your portfolio, and get financial and business news. As you can see in the figure on the left below, the bottom row is reserved for larger panels for more involved reports (options chains, major indices, a great news panel, a watch list, and a panel for your portfolio). The upper row (also in that figure) is made up of smaller panels (alerts, accounts, orders, transactions, transfers, charts, quotes, markets, and a panel for CNBC videos that only works for Power E*TRADE customers).

Both rows have navigation dots to show you where you are in that list — and you can independently scroll through them with a horizontal swipe. What's even cooler is that any panel with more information than you can see is also scrollable with a vertical swipe. In fact, the News panel has two columns, one for article titles and one for the actual articles, and both scroll independently of each other. It's slick, it makes sense, and it works, which is a great combination to me.

At the bottom of the screen in that same figure, you'll notice small buttons for Log Off, Menu, Accounts, Research, and Trading (you can also turn streaming on and off, or quickly enter a stock symbol to get that company's chart). These buttons pull up panels in both rows that work together, another thing I love about this app. For instance, the Research button pulls up the News panel in the bottom row and the Quotes and Market panels in the top row (in landscape mode, you get a third panel up top, but I preferred portrait mode). If you first selected a stock from your Watch List or Portfolio, all three panels will be specific to that stock — otherwise it defaults to general market news. The Accounts button brings up Portfolios, Alerts, and Accounts; the Menu button pulls up a pop-up window with a list of all included panels; and the Trading button pulls up a panel where you can quickly place an order, as you can see in the figure on the right below.

Now, most of these features require an E*TRADE account. You can't buy or sell stocks, for instance, without such an account, and you can't have a portfolio of stocks or get alerts, and so on. What you can do, however, is get stock quotes, company news articles, and see the stock indexes — even without an account.

Best features

I love the way E*TRADE made all the pieces fit together. If you're an E*Trade customer, I would be surprised if you went back to managing your account in a browser on a computer.

Worst features

You have to have an E*TRADE account to use all of the apps features. For those who don't, I'd recommend Stockwatch — iPad Edition (which I talk about below) for monitoring stocks and a portfolio.

StockSpy HD
$4.99

StockSpy HD is another app that caught my attention because it does something that's new to me, but before I get into that I'll describe the app overall. StockSpy allows you to track a portfolio of stocks and/or the major indices. In addition, you can add RSS feeds for individual companies (or indices) and then browse those feeds directly in the app.

That feature alone might have earned a mention, as this app is clean, easy to use, and convenient. It's where the developers married these two seemingly disparate ideas — news and stock prices — that StockSpy becomes more than just convenient, it becomes cool. StockSpy HD allows you to see exactly how the news affected a stock's price in stark visual terms. Now a lot of the time there won't really be all that strong a correlation between news and a stock's performance, but for some companies, or for the active (or even volatile) stock, the news surrounding that company has a frequent and direct impact on how its stock performs.

And I ask you, is there any company for which this is truer than it is for Apple? I've been covering Apple's financial news for more than 13 years, and I'll tell you the answer to that question is no.

Let's back up a bit and look at how the app works. When I first opened the app, I found it defaulted to listing Apple, Google, and the Dow. You can add as many companies as you'd like, and you'll find them listed in a column on the left side of the screen. On the right side is an RSS feed of the company's Facebook posts (for what that's worth), but we want to see the real stuff, so tap on a stock. I picked Apple, as you can see in the figure below. I've already entered a few RSS feeds for Apple (including several broader finance RSS feeds that are applied to all my stocks), and you'll see that I have a list of many articles that have something to do with Apple or mention the company's name in some way.

On the right side of the screen (this app works best in landscape mode), I have three charts. The top chart is a Candlestick chart (see the explanation of "candlesticks" in the Daily Stocks write-up above) of Apple's stock performance over the last seven or eight months. In the middle is another chart showing how many articles about Apple were pulled from my (small list of) RSS feeds, and at the bottom is a third chart showing the volume for the company's stock, color-coded for our convenience (green for a winning day, red for a losing day).

TIP

When you're viewing a particular stock, you can swipe through the panel in the upper-left corner of the screen for different views of that stock.

Now, do you see that yellow line that goes through all three charts? That's a timeline; you tap and drag it back and forth — and when you do, you're taken to the news of the day you stop on! Alternately, if you scroll through the news, the timeline is automatically taken to the day in question on the stock graphs. This is a very cool feature for looking back at a company's performance and trying to understand how events unfolded and the way they affected a company's stock.

It's a simple and direct way to see how the news is affecting a company's stock performance. If you're the type of person who likes trying to piece together the big picture out of disparate facts and events, you'll enjoy this app.

Best features

The core idea of showing news juxtaposed with stock performance is what I think is the coolest thing about this app.

Worst features

The app needs more customization — say, an option that shows a major index as one of the three charts offered.

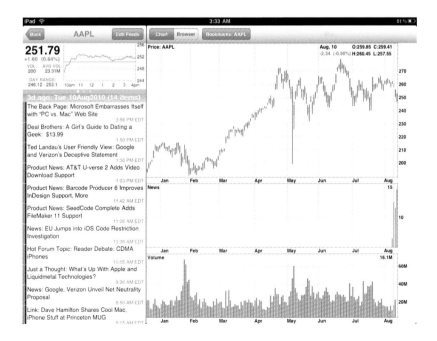

Stockwatch — iPad Edition
$5.99

As much as I like E*TRADE Mobile Pro for iPad, maybe you aren't an E*TRADE customer. Indeed, many investors use live brokers or other online brokers, and I know people who have investments through two or more brokerages. For all these people, Stockwatch — iPad Edition may be the best app for tracking the value of their portfolio(s).

To begin with, Stockwatch is a good-looking app. It's laid out well, and it offers some great features. For example, you can have a Watchlist for stocks you're watching that's separate from your portfolio. Better yet, you can have an unlimited number of portfolios — and each portfolio allows you to add an unlimited number of stocks and other symbols. Stockwatch will then allow you to track the value of your combined portfolios, or drill down to see how individual portfolios or stocks are doing.

Let's back up, though. The app defaults to the Watchlist view, which offers you a list of the stocks and indices you're tracking. You'll see the list of stocks, current trading information for whichever stock you've selected (including a graph), and a list of news stories relating to that stock. You can read the news stories through the in-app browser, too.

The Portfolios view gives you a great snapshot of your overall portfolio(s). In the figure below, you'll see a fake portfolio I wish I really had. I've got shares of Apple, AT&T, Google, and Citigroup (sure I do), along with shares in the Nasdaq 100 Trust (that's the QQQQ). Ugh, it's a down day for my portfolio, but overall my holdings are up more than 64%, so that's good!

At the upperleft is a panel for all my (fake) portfolios, and below that is a panel dedicated to the portfolio I am currently highlighting. For both, I get information on the total value, the total change in value, and the day's change in value, along with the base cost. Below those panels, I can see the individual stocks in that portfolio; if I tap one of those list items, I get current trading information, a graph of the day's action, and news relating to that stock.

For both the Watchlist and Portfolio, tap a graph to get a quick panel for changing the view and other features of that graph.

Better yet, if I've bought any one stock on multiple occasions, I can enter each lot as a separate entry, and Stockwatch will then do the math for me.

TIP

When entering or editing a stock lot in landscape mode, hide the keyboard to edit the acquisition date.

Stockwatch offers a wide array of preferences you can use to tweak your views and the format of your data. Most users will appreciate the defaults for all these preferences, but if you want things *just so*, Stockwatch is very tweakable.

Another nice feature is the capability to set a passcode for opening Stockwatch. This is above and beyond the main passcode for your iPad — meaning you can leave your device unlocked but still lock your financial data (alternatively, you can have two layers of security!). It's a nice touch.

Lastly, you can synch your data across multiple devices running Stockwatch!

Best features

Highly customizable and capable of great detail, Stockwatch is a great app for people with complex portfolios, especially if they want to track multiple portfolios from multiple brokerages.

Worst features

The version of Stockwatch I was testing was prone to crashing, but that's something I hope has been fixed by the time you read this.

Pageonce Personal Finance

Free (Ad-Supported) — Hybrid

Pageonce Personal Finance is a personal finance service aimed specifically at the mobile market, and this app is a hybrid app that will work on both iPhone and iPad. That app allows you to track your bills and expenses, monitor your credit cards, check your bank account status, check on your stocks, and track your frequent-flyer mileage programs. You can even remotely destroy your data through the service's Web site if you ever lose your iPhone or iPad. There's a Premium version of the app ($6.99) that is ad-free and offers additional features that fans are likely to be willing to pay for.

SplashMoney HD

$4.99

SplashMoney HD is a money management app for the iPad that allows you to monitor online banking accounts (checking, savings, etc.) and credit cards, create budgets, and track your actual spending (within those budgets, right?). You can synch data between the iPad app and the Mac or Windows version of the software, too, which is very handy. The app is designed well, is colorful, and provides attractive and informative graphs to help you visualize what you are doing with your money. It also includes an app-specific password option for additional security.

Thomson Reuters Marketboard

Free

Marketboard is a visually appealing app, and one that offers some nice features. For one thing, it offers a live scrolling look at all the major indices, and you can add stocks to a Watchlist for snapshot looks. In addition, Marketboard offers access to the company's extensive financial news coverage, and that alone will be worth the download for many users. The app also highlights recent earnings calls across the market, and allows you to purchase and view transcripts from those calls right there in the app. Transcripts won't appeal to everyone, but if you like to do that sort of research, you'll want Marketboard in your arsenal.

The Wall Street Journal
Free or Subscription

Arguably one of the most important business dailies on the planet, *The Wall Street Journal* is also a key element of parent company News Corp.'s efforts to monetize online content. That's why I listed the price as "Free or Subscription," because the price has been in flux while the company works on its strategy. Be that as it may, this is a solid app, and a great way to read *The Journal*. There are plenty of photographs, as well as some videos (provided by other News Corp. properties such as Fox News). There are also ads, even for paid subscribers, but the layout works.

XpenseTracker
$4.99 — Hybrid

As the name suggests, XpenseTracker allows you to track your expenses, both business and personal. It has some nice features — such as remembering your last payment transaction for each of the categories — and it supports all major currencies. Now, XpenseTracker isn't the only expense-tracking app in the App Store, but it is one of the few that supports Dropbox (but note that Dropbox support costs an extra $0.99 as an in-app purchase). That makes it is easy to import and export files from your computer — which can be the key to actually using an app like this effectively. After all, it doesn't make any difference how nifty an app is if you don't use it!

6 Food, Cooking, and Nutrition

Epicurious Recipes & Shopping List

Free (Ad-Supported)

There are apps based on Web sites and there are apps made by Web sites expressly for the iPad (and/or iPhone). Epicurious is one of the latter, an iPad/iPhone hybrid app that offers *some* content from the Web site. But what makes it stand out is the way it takes advantage of the iPad's multi-touch interface.

Epicurious is a recipe app "for people who love to eat." It's nicely laid out, easy to navigate, offers great photos of most of the finished dishes, and provides a shopping list feature that is super convenient. It also offers user reviews, many of which have suggestions on how to tweak the recipes. And many recipes tell you a little about the chef who created it. Better yet, some recipes even have nutritional information!

What's not to like?

Let's look a little at how to use it. The app offers several ways to browse for recipes. For instance, there are ten different categories, from Summer Dinners to Decadent Desserts. When you pick a category (Summer Dinners in the figure on the left below), the screen offers an easy-to-read list of the recipes in that category, with tabs on the far right that provide sorting options for the list.

Try using the Rating tab to see only the best recipes, or the Newest tab to see what's recently been added.

When you choose a recipe, you get a new page with easy-to-read directions on how to make it. In the image on the right below, you see the Ingredients as an overlay. This is how it works when your iPad is held in portrait mode. But the developers were clever — if you're viewing the app in landscape mode, the ingredients list appears on the main screen in its own panel (and not in a pop-up overlay). I love clever programming!

At the bottom of each Recipe screen are tabs for Reviews (those user reviews I mentioned) and About (info about the author); if the recipe offers nutritional information, you'll see a third tab for that.

Those features alone would make this a good recipe app, in my opinion — but there's more to Epicurious. There's a Search button so you can search for recipes in several ways: by Main Ingredient, Meal/Course, Cuisines, Dietary Consideration, Dish Type, and Season or Occasion. This makes finding the recipe you need nice and easy.

We're still not done, though, because there's also a shopping-list feature that I think is simply the bee's knees. Just tap a button and you get a shopping list with the precise amounts of everything you need to prepare that dish. If you include more than one recipe, you get one long list, broken down into sections for easier shopping.

Best features

Gorgeous pics, easy-to-read recipes, great navigation, an intuitive interface, the shopping list . . . it's hard to choose which feature I like best.

Worst features

The app currently doesn't allow you to sync the app to your online account at Epicurious.com. (On the other hand, you don't have to create or register an account to use the app!)

Grocery IQ
Free

Grocery IQ is, at its heart, a grocery-store-shopping-list app. A lot has changed with this app since it appeared in *Incredible iPhone Apps for Dummies* early in 2010 — and today the app is even better.

For one thing, it's now free. Plus, it has new features that I think are just terrific. They've added more items to its database, there's an awesome new coupon system, and you can now synch lists with other Grocery IQ users — which comes in handy if you have a wife, husband, significant other, or roommates who share the shopping duties.

To start a new list, tap the + button in the List tab, find an item, and you're off to the races. You can add items from your Favorites or History by tapping the Add to List button at the bottom of the item's entry page, too. In the figure on the left below, you'll see a grocery list I put together for a little cookout I'm putting on for some friends, with each item broken down by the aisle on which it's found.

You can add items, edit existing items, change aisle information, edit weights, add a description, or even add a note to every item in the database. This is something you'll probably want to do if you're going to regularly use the app.

In my hypothetical shopping trip here, I've already gotten dill pickles, mustard, and some cookies, so those items were moved to the bottom of my list. See the green bar near the bottom? That tells me I have four items in my basket, and that I still have ten more items to go. As items you've already gotten are moved out of the way, you'll do less scrolling and more looking at what you still need to buy. But if you want to go over what you've already put in your basket, that list is still right there, too.

Let me take a second to divert your attention to the figure on the right below. It's a list of coupons available to me right in the app (and I suspect a big reason the app is now free, as these are all supplied by Coupons.com). Since I'm planning on getting some cookies for this cookout, I "clipped" that Nabisco coupon. At that point I could have printed it on my networked HP printer or e-mailed it to myself to print. Better yet, Grocery IQ added the cookies to my list when I clipped the coupon, which serves as a nice reminder for me to take the coupon with me when I head off to the store! If you're like me, you probably forget coupons more often than you remember them, so I really like this feature.

When you're done shopping, all you have to do is tap the "Checkout" button and your list is cleared.

With list sharing, you can invite other users to share your list when you're shopping as a team. When any participant checks off an item, it's checked off on everyone else's list, too!

Favorites are very handy for items you often need to add to your shopping list. You can add items to your Favorites by tapping the Add to Favorites button on each item's entry page or by going to the Favorites tab, tapping the + button, and searching for the item. There's also a History tab that includes everything from your already-completed shopping lists, so you can easily add those items to a new list or to your Favorites.

There are several shopping apps for iPad (and iPhone), but Grocery IQ has a great look and feel — and the kind of features I actually wanted to use.

Best features

Grocery IQ has a huge database, and I just love that items are broken down by aisle.

Worst features

List sharing requires accepting Coupons.com's terms of service, and that means there's one more party with access to some of my information. If this bothers you, don't register and don't use list sharing.

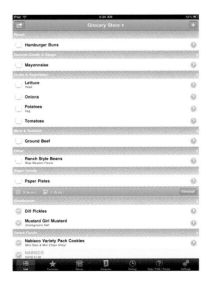

Urbanspoon for iPad
Free

How many times have you spent 45 minutes playing the "I don't know, where do *you* want to go?" game with your spouse, your friends, or your workmates? I hate that game, and I can't even begin to tell you how much, but Urbanspoon can change that.

The basic premise of the app is to let you find a restaurant by randomly choosing from various cuisines, price points, and different neighborhoods on three slot machine reels. Shake your iPad (or push the "Shake" button) and you get a random suggestion for where to eat. If you don't like the result, shake it again. If you want to limit your options, say to a particular neighborhood or a type of food, you can lock one, two, or even all three reels to try and find a particular kind of restaurant.

 Check out the "Show Popular" button at the top left of the map to limit your choices to only restaurants that have been highly rated by Urbanspoon users, as I have done in the figure on the left below.

When you get a restaurant you like, just tap its name and you'll see a screen with its address, phone number, kind of restaurant, Urbanspoon user rating, cost rating (indicated by one, two, or three dollar signs), and reviews of the place (where applicable). In the case of Delfina, which you can see in the figure on the right below, there's a critic's review from the *San Jose Mercury News* and other newspapers, some blog posts, and several user reviews.

Tap various items on the screen to reveal details such as hours, a menu (sometimes), more about the restaurant's user rating (such as how many people voted), the opportunity to submit your own rating, suggestions of other restaurants you might like, an advertisement (it's an ad-supported app), and directions from Google Maps.

 If you like or hate a place, make sure to write your own review, and think about the kind of things you find helpful in a review because "THIS PLACE ROCKS!" isn't all that useful.

Speaking of Google Maps, it's embedded right in the app. When you're viewing in Map mode, all results come up on the map that dominates two-thirds of your screen. When you Shake for a restaurant, the map zooms to that location's neighborhood, with the selected restaurant and other restaurants nearby represented by pins in the map. This makes it easy to take a quick look at what other options you have in that neighborhood. Conversely, when you select a pin on the map, the slot machine reels rotate to match that restaurant. This also makes for quick identification, and I like that kind of attention to detail.

Another cool feature on maps is that the more popular a restaurant is, the darker the shade of blue that identifies its pin — and the restaurant currently selected has a bright red pin. I love these subtle visual clues.

Using the map to display the results this way cuts a couple of steps out of the process of using Urbanspoon for iPad. I'm a visual learner, and this is the sort of thing that helps me.

There's a list mode, as well, but it only shows the most popular restaurants in the city you're looking at.

 If you're adventuresome, try limiting yourself to one shake and sticking to whatever comes up. It could be awful, but you might also discover a new restaurant you wouldn't have tried otherwise. Come on, try it!

Best features

The large map works for me, and I found it makes it a lot easier to browse restaurants by neighborhood.

Worst features

The iPad version of this app is lacking some features from the iPhone version; for example, it can't filter out restaurant chains.

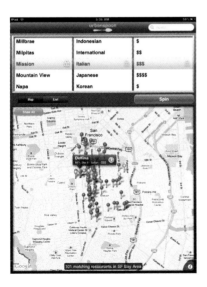
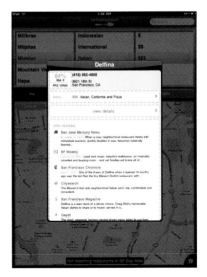

Weber's on the Grill for iPad
$4.99

I love this app, and so do the people who have downloaded it on the App Store (and that's saying something). It has a lot of recipes for grilling and BBQ-ing, and those recipes have gorgeous pictures and easy-to-follow directions. But there's more (and it's the "more" that I think sets this app apart), most especially a series of How-Tos that covers everything from grilling basics to individual cooking techniques. Even better still is that some of those How-To's are videos created by celebrity chef and cookbook author Jamie Purviance.

Fire up Weber's on the Grill (Get it? Fire up? Yep, I thought that was funny), and you'll be treated to several photographs of delicious-looking food — including a pizza! (Who knew you could make pizza on a grill?). If you're holding your iPad in landscape mode, you'll have a list on the left side of the screen, as shown in the figure on the left below. If you're holding your iPad in portrait mode, you'll have to tap the Contents button first. Either way, the list defaults to Recipes. But you can also tap to the How-Tos and Groceries buttons at the bottom to peruse that content.

Let's start with the Recipes, the *raison d'être* of this app. You can browse by category, such as Starters, Red Meat, Seafood, Rubs, Marinades, and such, or search for ingredients or other keywords.

Pick a category — say, Red Meat — and the category list becomes a list of recipes in that category. I scrolled down until I found a recipe called Hoison Beef Kabobs that I can't wait to try! And Filet Mignon with Shoestring Potatoes (not shown)? Boy, they look great!

Every picture in this app can be tapped once to see a larger version. This isn't just for aesthetics; sometimes you need to see the larger image to check out some detail in the presentation, or maybe to better understand the technique in the How-To photos.

In any event, tap a recipe and it appears on the screen. You're told how many the recipe serves, how much prep time you'll need, how much time for marinating or other post-prep, grilling time, and a list of any special equipment (like bamboo skewers) you might need. There's also a detailed ingredient list, a photo of the finished dish, and step-by-step instructions for making the dish. Those instructions even include a breakdown of individual timed steps when the timing is important.

At the top of each recipe is an icon for adding it to your Favorites, generating a shopping list, or e-mailing it out to someone else.

Let's move on the "More" bit and look at those How-To's. Most of them are a combination of step-by-step instructions and photographs for each step. If you've ever wondered how to peel a shrimp, what a chimney starter is, or how to use a chimney starter, you'll find more than 100 How-Tos that answer those questions and many more.

As I said earlier, some of the How-Tos contain videos by Jamie Purviance, who is really good at showing you just how to do the things he makes look so easy. From cooking a chicken on a beer can to trimming spareribs in a St. Louis-Style Cut, his videos are great. I should note, however, that a couple of the videos have a lot of wind noise from an improperly shielded microphone. They're a rarity, though, so if you hit one of those first, know that the rest of them are very high-quality.

Videos are marked with a little video-camera icon in the list so you can know which is which.

Best features

The photos, the instructions, and the How-Tos, especially those videos, are what make this app worth every penny.

Worst features

You can't synch grocery lists between the iPhone and iPad versions of this app. In addition, though the videos are great, there's a lot of disparity in the audio quality from video to video, and sometimes the audio even sounds distorted.

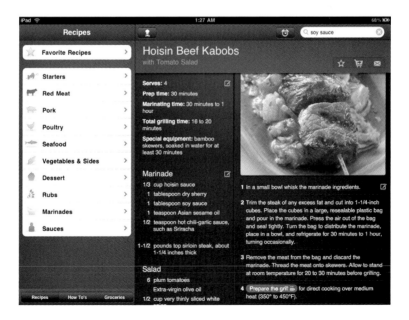

ZAGAT TO GO

$9.99 per year

I like Urbanspoon, and Yelp does that Yelp thing like nobody else can, but what if you want to find a restaurant based on more professional criteria? ZAGAT offers reviews compiled by professional editors based on customer surveys, and in an age where budget-constrained newspapers are cutting back on local coverage such as restaurant reviews, ZAGAT is the kind of resource that will only become more valuable as time goes on, especially with iOS devices.

ZAGAT is one of the most comprehensive restaurant guides on the planet, and this hybrid iPhone, iPod touch, and iPad app gives you access to thousands of restaurant reviews, a GPS-enabled restaurant locator, the ability to search for restaurants according to multiple criteria, and more. This is definitely a must-have app for foodies, and unlike the print version, the app is constantly updated with new reviews.

ZAGAT is limited to major metropolitan areas. That means you should check to make sure the areas where you'll use it the most are actually covered.

ZAGAT TO GO allows you to pick a major city, or use your iPad's Location Services to determine your current location. The interface itself is almost entirely dominated by a Google Maps display of the area, with ZAGAT-reviewed restaurants highlighted with "Z" pins, as you can see in the figure on the left below. Tap a pin and you'll get a panel at the top of the screen with basic information about the place — including its name, its Food, Décor, and Service rating on a scale of 0–30, along with the average cost of a meal (including one drink and a tip). You'll also find the beginning of the ZAGAT review, which will often be enough to let you know if you want to eat there.

Tap the panel, and you get a full-screen workup on the restaurant. This includes the hours of operation, features of the restaurant, address and phone number, an e-mail link, and the capability to drop the contact information directly to your Address Book! I really like that feature, and I hope to see it make its way to more apps in the future.

What's with all those quotes in a ZAGAT review? The company's editors compile their reviews from customer surveys, and they use (very) short quotes from those surveys throughout their reviews.

There's also a Star icon for adding the restaurant to your Favorites, and a little "i" (for "information") icon you can press to see an explanation of ZAGAT's review system, as shown in the figure on the right below.

ZAGAT uses a 30-point scale; if you're not familiar with just what those numbers mean, this is a very handy explanation that's just a tap away.

If you don't want to browse restaurants from a map, tap the icon that looks like six little boxes at the bottom of the screen to browse local restaurants in list form. You can sort by Food, Décor, and Service ratings, by cost, or alphabetically. Just swipe the screen to go to the next page, and tap any of the eight listing on each page to get the full screen work-up we mentioned above.

Note that you'll need a connection to the Internet to make the most use this app; it pulls reviews from the company's servers. You can, however, view reviews in your History and Favorites without a connection.

Whether you are looking for a great place for an anniversary dinner, an appropriate place to pitch your business proposal to a prospective investor, or want to find great places to eat when you're traveling, ZAGAT TO GO will be an invaluable app for your iPad.

Best features

Crowd-sourcing can be great, but sometimes I like the more edited and professional approach to finding a restaurant that I get with ZAGAT TO GO.

Worst features

I'd like having the capability to store a map of the area around me for offline viewing — the entire area, and not just the restaurants I've looked at in the past.

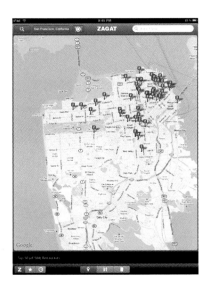
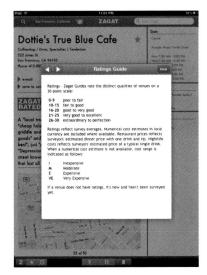

170,000+ Recipes — Big Oven Lite (or Pro)

Free (or $9.99 for the Pro version)

This app serves as an iPad-interface for BigOven.com, a recipe-and-cuisine Web site. There are now more than 170,000 recipes available, and the iPad version of this app offers a great way to browse all that content. You can rate each recipe, and there are features like "Try Soon Recipes," the "Leftover Wizard," "What's for Dinner," and the "Random Recipe." There's a lot of content on BigOven.com, and if you're a foodie you'll like this app. There is a free version that is ad-supported, and a Pro version for $9.99 that adds such features as a grocery-list generator, a log of recipes you've made, a food glossary, and more.

Health Food Store Locator

$2.99

Food consciousness has probably never been higher than it is today, and the success of Whole Foods, Trader Joe's, and other stores that sell "health food" can attest to that. Still, finding a store that specializes in organic and other health foods can be hard — especially when you travel — but Health Food Store Locator can change that. It uses Google Maps to find only the stores in this category, and you can filter the results by proximity to your location or a particular Zip code. This app isn't particularly pretty, but if you want an easy way to find a health food store, it'll do the trick.

iCanEat OnTheGo Gluten & Allergen Free

$2.99

This app is aimed at a narrow market — those with food allergies or celiac — but for those whom it affects, the topic is important. The app features some 20 different fast-food chains, and for each one, you can enter your food allergens and tap to find menu items you can eat. It tracks nine allergens — eggs, fish, gluten, milk, peanuts, shellfish, soy, tree nuts, and wheat — and you can toggle those in any combination you need. The app includes a subset of 14 chains that provide information relating to gluten content. If you have food allergies and eat fast food, you'll want this app.

Where To Eat? Find restaurants using GPS
$2.99

Where To Eat? is another restaurant finder I like. It uses Google Maps to show you all the restaurants near where you search — and it can use Location Services to figure out where you are. Users can rate restaurants, and those ratings get compiled for all users to see; you can also flag a location as being closed, get directions, and share restaurants via e-mail. The app gives you a couple of ways to browse by category, and includes a tip calculator if you need a little help with the math. The interface is clean; you might like it if you think that Yelp or Urbanspoon are too cluttered.

Wiki Cocktail Machine HD
Free

I have to lead off this look at Wiki Cocktail Machine HD with a moment of full disclosure: I don't drink. Maybe you do, however. I have plenty of friends who agreed with me that this app is a fun way to find alcoholic drink recipes, especially at parties. The main feature is a randomizer — Push the Shake button and you get a random drink, complete with a photograph, ingredients, and directions. You can also browse by Taste, Spirit, or Name, and you can set the measurements to be either Imperial (by the ounce) or Metric. With 62 recipes, the only thing it needs is more recipes.

7 Games

 ## Angry Birds HD
$4.99

When I first heard about Angry Birds for the iPhone, I thought it sounded stupid. It *is* stupid. The object is to shoot birds from a slingshot-like apparatus to knock down structures and kill the green pigs who have stolen the birds' eggs. Kill all the green pigs on a level and you get to advance, but leave even one little green piggy alive and you'll have to try this level again.

It's a simple premise with a plot as old as time, goofy animation, and a boppin' theme song you'll hum for days. And while it doesn't sound particularly appealing on paper, almost everyone I know who is playing Angry Birds on their iPhone or their iPad says it's their favorite game ever. And having played most of its levels, I, too, find it totally addicting.

The birds are your weapons. On each level you get a fixed number of birds; use the birds to kill all the pigs. Aim your bird carefully and be sure you don't pull back the slingshot too much or too little. Different birds have different attributes. Little blue birds, for example, divide into three individual blue birds when you tap while they're in flight. The yellow triangular birds double their speed when you tap while they're flying. The big white egg-shaped birds drop an egg-shaped bomb when you tap. All three of these bird types can be seen in the image below.

Remember, your primary objective may be to destroy the pigs using the fewest missiles (birds), but you'll usually have to destroy structures and other stuff to get to the pigs. It will behoove you to pay careful attention to the physics for each level. Note that ice is easier to shatter than wood; wood is easier to pierce than metal; birds have trouble moving or damaging metal; and TNT pretty much blows the heck out of pretty much everything near it.

There are 180 levels to date — and they're all physics-based puzzles that require a combination of logic, skill, luck, and brute force. The developer has released content updates regularly, with new levels and, occasionally, a new bird type.

I was surprised to find myself playing long after I had planned to quit. I'd think, "I'll just beat this level and then go to sleep." Then I'd beat the level and think, "I'll just beat one more level before I go to sleep." The next thing I know, it's 1:00 a.m. and there I am, still playing "one more level" of Angry Birds.

It's just one of those games that makes you want to try it "just one more time" every time you try it. It's a little bit goofy but it's extremely challenging and enjoyable.

Best features

There are a lot of levels — 180 at last count — so it keeps you hooked for a good, long time. And the developer has hinted at new levels in the future.

Worst features

I can't get the stupid song out of my head.

Pinball HD
$2.99 US

I own half a dozen iPhone pinball games, and the one I enjoy the most and find has the most replay value is The Deep Pinball. And before The Deep Pinball came out, its developer's first release, Wild West Pinball (99¢), was my favorite pinball app and is still a close second. Jungle Style Pinball, also from the same developer, was another of my favorite iPhone games.

Yes, I'm talking about *iPhone* games, not iPad games, but bear with me here for a minute.

Good pinball games require supremely realistic physics — and all three of the iPhone Pinball games I mentioned nail it. The way the ball moves around the table and interacts with bumpers and flippers is completely realistic and authentic. So realistic, in fact, that you can "shake" the table to influence the ball's movement. And like a real pinball machine, if you shake too hard, you'll tilt and lose your ball. Furthermore, I sometimes get so involved in my game that I use body English, thrusting a hip or shoulder forward as I shake my iPhone, which my wife finds hysterically funny.

Another hallmark of a great pinball game is great sound effects, and those three aforementioned pinball games don't disappoint. The sounds the ball makes when it bounces off a bumper, is hit with a flipper, or passes through a rollover are spot-on and totally authentic.

Okay. So here's how that relates to Pinball HD for the iPad: The developer of all three iPhone pinball games combined them into a single incredible iPad app called Pinball HD. They're all there — The Deep, Wild West Pinball, and Jungle Style Pinball — and better than even their fabulous iPhone predecessors.

One thing I hate about some pinball games is that they don't let you know your current objective, what happens when you hit specific targets or rollovers, or what targets you should be aiming for right now. All three tables in Pinball HD offer an instruction page (Jungle Style's is shown in the figure to the left below) that explains your objectives and offers detailed advice about specific features of the table such as the sunken boat in The Deep (shown on the right below). Without this instruction page, I might have never realized that switching off the whirlpool opened up access to the sunken ship.

I like that you can play all three tables in your choice of either the "full-table view," as shown on the right below, or a "flying-table" view where the virtual camera follows the ball around, zooming and panning to show you the action up close and personal. And I liked having the option to play in either portrait or landscape mode.

The tables are all masterpieces. The graphics are unbelievably realistic and the ball physics will absolutely blow your mind. That said, I find one of the games — The Deep — more challenging than the others. I think Wild West and Jungle Style Pinball are trying harder to look and feel like old-school pinball machines while The Deep seems to revel in its digital-ness and care less about emulating a machine from another era.

All three tables are fun, and it's a great showcase for your iPad's speedy processor and graphics.

Best features

Great ball and table physics, combined with killer sound effects, make for thoroughly enjoyable and realistic pinball simulations.

Worst features

One table is decidedly more fun than the other two.

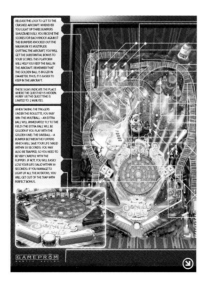

Pocket Legends

Free

If you're a fan of MMORPG-style gaming, I'm happy to inform you that Pocket Legends for iPad is an incredibly cool 3D MMO game that doesn't (or at least doesn't have to) cost you a cent.

For those who aren't already fans of the genre, MMORPG is the acronym for Massively-Multiplayer Online Role-Playing Game.

What that means is that you can join thousands of players from all over the world when you play. You begin by choosing one of three character classes to play as: an archer, an enchantress, or a warrior. Then you (and, optionally, other players) wander around dungeons, forests, and castles killing zombies, skeletons, demons, and other bad guys while collecting gold pieces, experience points, weaponry, and armor. In the game, your character frequently finds gold and experience points — and occasionally finds weapons, armor, and shields. Or you can buy weapons and armor with the gold you find. The longer you play, the more powerful your character becomes — and the more powerful the weapons, armor, and shields you are able to use.

In the beginning, you'll "level up" quickly, which may be why this game calls to me when I'm doing something productive . . . "Come on tough guy . . . Kill a few zombies and reach level 22 . . . ." It may also be why I often succumb to its calling.

But even if you're completely antisocial, don't worry — it's even fun to play alone. That said, it's a lot more fun to gang up on the bad guys with a group — you gain more power (and gain it faster) when you play in a group than when you play solo. Players are magically dropped into games, joining players with similar skills. In the figure below I (Doc) am shooting at a bad guy while my associates — Oswad, Yoggiee, Racecardude, and Xxbloodyxx — are battling other nogoodniks and plundering chests full of gold.

The bottom line is that very few games deliver this much fun, look this good, and are this addicting. Give it a shot — you have nothing to lose but a few minutes (or hours) of time.

By the way, the reason I said "doesn't have to cost you money" rather than the more absolute "doesn't cost you money" back there in the first paragraph is that if you enjoy playing it (as I do), you'll probably want to purchase additional dungeon campaigns ($1.99 each), gold (2,500 pieces for $2.99), additional characters (just $0.99 each), or one of the other goodies that are available for in-app purchase. You don't have to — you can have a lot of fun for a good long time without laying out a dime — but if you like playing, you'll probably find yourself considering a purchase or two.

Here is one last thing: My characters are an archer named Doc and an Enchantress named Levitusaurus. So if you happen to run into me in a dungeon or forest, use the chat system to give me a shout-out.

Best features

Easy to learn and still fun after 22 levels. The details in this gorgeous iPad game are superb, and the iPad screen makes them a pleasure to look at. Plus it's free.

Worst features

If you zoom in so you can really enjoy the details, you will die a thousand horrible deaths at the hands of creatures you can no longer see. Too bad it's an either/or proposition: You can admire the awesome graphical detail or you can zoom out and live through some battles, but not both.

Real Racing HD
$9.99

At least a dozen car-race games are available for the iPad already, but Real Racing is the real deal. With 48 cars in 4 classes, 12 tracks, and 5 unique game modes, a career mode with 3 divisions and 76 events, plus multiplayer Wi-Fi support for as many as 6 racers, it'll take you a good long time to master it. Heck, it'll take you a good long time to unlock all the different tracks and cars, let alone master the game!

One thing I really like about Real Racing is that, unlike many other racing games, it offers a myriad of options for controlling your race car. You can steer by accelerometer (tilting the iPhone) or by touching the left or right side of the screen. You can accelerate either automatically or manually. And you can adjust the accelerometer and brake sensitivity. Because you can fine-tune these controls, playing Real Racing is a lot more fun than playing other games that offer fewer control options.

Another thing I like is the number of game-play options. For example, if you like racing against real people, you can compete against up to five friends over Wi-Fi. Or you can participate in one of the online leagues and advance to a higher division if you're any good. League play is open only to players after they've achieved some measure of success in their single-player Real Racing career, so there aren't a lot of novices. This makes league play more enjoyable and challenging. I know I always get my butt whopped.

If you don't want to race real humans, there is still a race mode for every occasion. If you've only got a few minutes, try a three-lap Quick Race against five computer-controlled drivers. Or choose to compete in a Time Trial, where your only opponent is the ticking clock. Check out the Ghost Racing mode, where you chase a ghost image of your car's best lap time. As you develop skills, you'll try to keep the ghost image from passing you. It's fun. Finally, there's the career mode, which is guaranteed to take you a long time to complete, with its 76 events. With new tracks and new cars that you unlock when you win, there's always something new and you never get bored.

The sound effects are great; the tracks are unique; and there are a variety of different driving surfaces such as asphalt, grass, gravel, and ripple-strips, each with its own effect on your car's speed and handling.

The driving experience is quite realistic. A good example is that when you tap the brake, your car slows down, but it also downshifts to a lower gear and handles a little better.

One quick tap right before a sharp turn or chicane is better than pressing and holding or multiple taps of the brakes.

I recommended Real Racing when it first came out. Just check out some of its reviews in the App Store. There must be a good reason for its 4.5 out of 5-star rating and thousands of positive reviews.

Best features

The best thing about Real Racing is that it delivers a lot of variety in its control options, tracks, cars, and race modes against both computer and real opponents.

Worst features

Occasional network errors can spoil online races.

Scene It? Comedy Movies
$4.99

I have to admit that Scene It? Comedy Movies was my tenth (last) choice for this chapter. There were a lot of really incredible games that didn't make the cut, but I really think you'll like this game for its varied uses of the touch-screen interface, in spite of its shortcomings.

The game is, of course, about comedy movies, primarily of the last 25 years. The format is a game-show-style quiz with questions presented in a variety of ways, as I'll explain. But first, the big picture: The game has three play modes — Table Play, where 1 to 4 players share the same iPad; Multiplayer Play, where up to 4 players (on up to 4 iPads) duke it out; plus 20 single-player games. Each game asks 20 or 30 trivia questions about Hollywood comedies and their stars — presented in various formats and timed. The longer it takes you to answer, the fewer points you score.

The best parts are the Funny Bits questions. Each starts with a video clip from a well-known comedy, followed by several questions about the clip. Pay close attention — one of the questions could be something like, "What was the first line in that clip?" or "What office hours did the teacher mention in this scene?" Whether I've seen the movie or not, I usually get a chuckle out of these clips.

Another type of question shows you a film poster, but through the miracle of modern multimedia, its elements appear one element at a time as shown in the figure below. The bomb at bottom right that says "210" is the clock ticking. When it started (at 300) all you saw was the sky. Then, with around 140 remaining, the rest of the graphics appeared, and with only a few seconds left, all the type (including the movie title) appeared. (Extra credit: Guess what movie the incomplete poster below is from?)

Recipe for Comedy questions are fun, too. The "ingredients" are revealed one at a time, with the bomb (clock) counting down quickly. Other question formats include these:

- ✔ **Who Am I questions:** Name the actor as facts about him or her are revealed one at a time.
- ✔ **Punchline:** Supply the next line of dialog after watching an incomplete video clip.

✔ **Invisibles:** Name the actor by looking at a still image of a movie scene, but with the actors heads' removed.

✔ **Tumble Together Quotes:** Pick the right words to finish a quote from a specified film.

✔ **Pixel Flicks:** Name the movie by watching a low-tech pixelated animation that tells you the story (or should) .

✔ **Sorting puzzles:** Drag words and phrases onto the appropriate movie poster.

I don't like some other puzzles that have you rub the screen to reveal an image or hunt for a tiny image among a *lot* of tiny images. If you can forgive those shortcomings (and I have), this movie-trivia game is a ton of fun.

Best features

This is one of a very few iPad games I can interest my whole family in playing, and everyone agrees it's fun.

Worst features

Not enough games for $5 (we had seen all the questions within a couple of hours of play) and not enough video clips in the games.

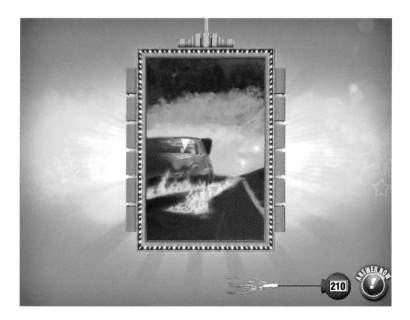

Crosswords
$9.99

The trouble with most other crossword-puzzle apps is that they either have crummy puzzles or they charge money for the puzzles — a la carte or by subscription. The Crosswords app uses a different model. For your $10 you continuously receive new puzzles from sources that include *Houston Chronicle, Washington Post, New York Times Classic Crosswords,* and many others. And of course it has a very usable interface, designed for both landscape and portrait modes.

If you're feeling smug, look in the Information screen for the puzzle to see how quickly others have solved it.

Flight Control HD
$4.99

This is another one of those games that doesn't sound great in theory but is a blast to play. And you'll want to play again and again . . . I guarantee it. You're the air traffic controller for a map-full (there are eight maps) of airports, aircraft carriers, and helipads. Aircraft appear on all four edges of the screen. Your job is to land them all safely by drawing their paths to landing. Did I mention that aircraft and landing spot must be the same color? Or that the aircraft come faster and there are more of them as the game progresses? It's a great game.

Pool Pro Online 3
$0.99

It's enough like real pool to be challenging and fun. It's easy to learn and difficult to master, a winning combo for games. Playing solo against computerized opponents is fun — but for a real challenge, head for one of the online lobbies of available players and hustle up a game. I strongly recommend that you practice on the solo levels — and practice a lot — before you go after any humans. Either way, the game controls are fluid and intuitive. And you'll get the hang of shots, even the ones that need some finesse, before you know it.

Tetris
$7.99

Tetris has been around for more than 25 years and I like this incarnation a lot. Tetris, if you aren't old enough to remember Clara Peller, was the first really popular falling-block game for personal computers. The first version I played had monochrome graphics and ran on a Mac Plus. This rendition's great — with a ghost image that helps you put blocks where you want them, and new power-ups and other stuff you may or may not consider an improvement. However you like it — classic or with new and improved features — it has a hypnotic quality that will keep you coming back for more.

Words With Friends HD
$2.99

It's a lot like Scrabble, but played against your friends or random strangers asynchronously. You make a word, then it's your opponent's turn. When your opponent makes a word, it's your turn again. Repeat until no tiles remain in your rack(s). It has all of your favorite Scrabble features — including double- and triple-word and letter scores. And the tiles have the same point value as in Scrabble, so you already know how to play! And you can play up to 20 games at a time.

8 Healthcare & Fitness

3D4Medical's Images — iPad Edition

Free

3D4Medical's Images — iPad Edition is little more than a bunch of gorgeous pictures of various parts of the human body, along with a few images pertaining to the health-care industry. These images and photos are so high quality and look so good on the iPad's display, it's hard to believe this app is free, but really it's a gateway app for 34DMedical.com's paid apps, which go into great detail about specific parts of the human body and include a lot of medi-cal information. I added it to this chapter about Healthcare & Fitness apps because it's a great introduction to what the human body (and some microorganisms, too) looks like.

Navigation in this app is very straightfor-ward. The home page contains thumbnails of every image, and you can swipe up and down to see more. Tap a thumbnail to see the full image, and you're off.

3D4Medical's Images has several conceptual images of the male repro-ductive system, and a couple of images of the female breast (though oddly, there aren't any images of the female reproductive system). If you're sensitive to that sort of thing, you may want to skip this app.

A lot of these images are conceptual, and there are several different kinds of views included. From photographs of microscopic creatures to X-ray-like views of the different layers in our bodies, these images were all chosen for their impact, rather than to be a systematic look at the human body. There are also some images of pills that will remind some of the ongoing healthcare debate in the U.S., and there's a clear message that smoking is bad for you. Most of the images, however, are close-ups of muscles, bones, joints, and more.

When you're looking at a full image, you can tap it to pull up a panel that gives you the title of the image and a (too-) brief description. You can also save any of the images to your photo library to use as wallpaper on your iPad, or share the images through e-mail, Facebook, or Twitter (each with a link to the company's site). Tap the photo again, and the panel goes away. To view the next photo, just swipe to the left or right.

There's an "i" button in the bottom right, as you can see in the figure below. Tap that and you get buttons for a searchable index, a dedicated search button, a button for starting a slideshow of all the images, and a link back to the Home page, which is the thumbnail gallery. When your slideshow starts, just tap the screen again to make it stop.

If you're interested in beginning an exploration of the human body, you should check out this app.

Best features

This app is all about the gorgeous, high-quality photos.

Worst features

It needs more information about each photo than is currently provided. While the one or two lines that accompany each photo provide enough to tell you what it is, I'd love more contextual information.

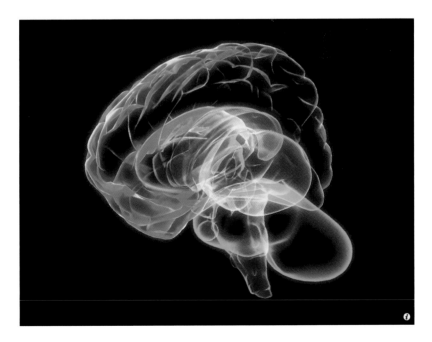

All-in YOGA HD: 200 Poses & Yoga Classes
$4.99

I'm not going to sit here and tell you that I'm some kind of yoga expert, because I'm not. Fortunately, All-in YOGA HD has the tools and information to help me, a yoga novice, and experienced yoga practitioners alike. It has a database of 200 poses with images and instructions on how to perform the poses, two built-in programs that will custom-build a routine to match your abilities, goals, and time commitment, the option to build your own routines, a journaling feature that tracks your workouts, and a very good in-app Help system. All those features make this app the best Yoga app I've seen on an iOS device.

The app includes 200 poses, and the developers divided them up by skill level — Beginner, Intermediate, Advanced, and Guru — along with an All view. Each skill level has two rows of poses that you can scroll through with a swipe. When you tap on a pose, you get directions for the pose, a photo of how the pose should look (tap it to see a larger version), and an audio button (tap it and a voice will read the description to you). Most of them also have a tappable video showing the pose in action. These instructions make understanding the pose pretty easy, even to a newbie like me.

The main poses have a 3D muscle view (shown on the left below) that shows you which muscles are stretched when doing that pose, as you can see in the figure to the left below. This helps me understand exactly which muscles are going to be killing me the day after I learn a new pose!

The app also offers workout programs, including Quick Recipes for ready-made workouts and a Personal Yoga Teacher that will design a workout for you based on your age, weight, goal, level, style, and how long you want to work out. You can also assemble your own workout by tapping from the database of poses and building exactly the routine you want. All three of these methods are easy to use and follow.

When you start a workout, you see a large image of the pose with a countdown timer for how long you should spend doing it. A voice offers instructions, music plays, and when it's time to move to the next, the image changes and the timer resets. There are onscreen controls for pausing the program, instructions for the current pose, turning off the voice or music, and for poses with a video, watching that video, all of which you can see in the figure on the right below. It's pretty straightforward, like the rest of the app.

One of the things I like a lot about this app is that it allows you to download all the audio and video content after installing the app on your iPad. Otherwise the app only downloads content as you need it.

If you do Yoga on your own, this app will be an invaluable tool.

Best features

A great layout, clear photographs and instructions, and the workout programs make this a great Yoga app.

Worst features

The most I can come up with to complain about is that not every pose has video and most don't have the awesome muscle views.

Eye Chart Premium
$1.99

Time out for a true story: During World World II, my grandfather went to join the Army. His vision was so bad he failed the (not-all-that-stringent) vision test given to would-be soldiers. So he did what any other fella would do — he memorized the eye chart, went down to the Navy, and passed that test with flying colors. Nigh on 70 years later, it turns out there's an app even for that, because with Eye Chart Premium, eye doctors can randomize the order of the letters or symbols in an eye chart to prevent such shenanigans.

Eye Chart Premium includes three different eye charts, the Snellen Chart, which you can see in the figure to the left below, Tumbling E Chart, and Landolt C Chart. I imagine most people reading this will be most familiar with the Snellen Chart that includes the letters E, F, P, T, O, L, C, and D. The top letter is huge, and each line below it gets progressively smaller. Each of those lines has a corresponding measure of basic eyesight acuity, you know, like 20/20 (so-called "perfect vision"). When viewed from 9 feet 11 inches away, it's a quick and easy way to measure your eyesight.

Then there's the Tumbling E Chart, which is used for patients who can't read (which is why it is also sometimes called the Illiterate E Chart), for young children, or when there's a language barrier. This chart is comprised only of the letter "E" that points in all four cardinal directions. The Landolt C Chart is similar; it uses the letter "C" facing in four directions.

The app also features a Mirror option that reverses the text in the chart, as you can see in the figure to the right below. This allows optometrists with small testing rooms to hold the test up to a mirror that is five feet away (hey, I'm neither a doctor nor a mathematician, so whatever half of 5'11" is!) and have the patient read the chart in the mirror. In my experience, this is a common aspect of many optometrists' offices, and it's the main reason to get Eye Chart Premium (the paid version) over Eye Chart Pro (the free version).

Now, you can use this chart to test yourself, and it's clear from the iTunes reviews on this app that many people get the free version for just that reason. But it seems that some doctors are interested in it, too, and that could be for its ability to randomize the letters, because you can switch back and forth quickly between the different charts, and the iPad's display is frankly superior to a projector on a white wall, at least in my (non-doctor's) opinion.

There's a Randomize button for the whole chart, but you can also tap an individual line to randomize just that line.

I suspect that the iPad (along with some of its competitors) will become increasingly common in doctors' offices, both for the doctor's own use and for use with patients. I thought this one was a clever idea for an app, and it might just be the kind of thing we see more of in the future.

Best features

I like the ability to randomize the tests, and having all three tests a tap away seems convenient.

Worst features

There are other charts used by optometrists that are not included in this app.

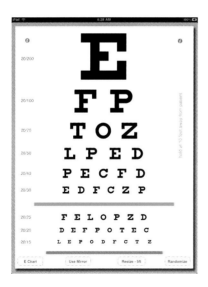
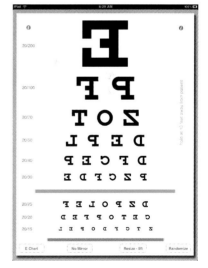

iFitness HD
$4.99

Here's an app I've always needed — iFitness HD has more than 300 exercises in it, and you can use it to track your workouts, your weight and/or size (whether you're trying to get bigger or smaller), and it includes a built-in Body Mass Index (BMI) Calculator. In short, it includes just about everything you need.

This app's standout feature, however, is its photographs and instructions on how to do the exercises and use all those machines in your gym. And if you're like me, you've found yourself in a gym more than once scratching your head and staring at some machine or other trying to figure out what it does and how to use it. With iFitness HD, you get those answers without having to pay for a personal trainer.

iFitness HD supports multiple profiles so more than one person can track workouts. To switch between profiles, just give your iPad a shake. That's handy!

In the Exercises tab, exercises are grouped according to abdominals, arms, back, chest, legs, and shoulders, as well as cardio exercises and stretches. You can also view them grouped according to specific muscles, as you can see in the figure to the left below, where I have the Pectoralis muscle picked. All the exercises that target that specific muscle are listed on the right side of the screen.

You can also see exercises grouped according to the equipment used. I think this is a great feature that allows me to make the most of whatever equipment I have on hand, especially if that selection of equipment is limited.

Going back to those chest exercises, tapping any of the exercises listed moves the list to the left side of the screen with the details of that exercise on the right, as you can see in the figure to the right below. You get photos for each of the major positions in the exercise, information on which muscles are worked, the skill level of that exercise, and step-by-step instructions that include details on how to use any equipment that's involved.

Some exercises have videos, which are really good for seeing how to do it right. You can save videos you've already watched with a setting under the More tab. This allows you to watch them later, which is handy if you're going to be working out somewhere without a WiFi network.

Once you know your exercises, you can choose from built-in routines that are designed for users of different levels and goals. There are also routines built for specific sports (like golf and hockey), or for targeting specific parts of the body. You can also build your own routine and assemble whatever exercises you want to do.

You can record weight and reps for each exercise — the results of which are logged and graphed if you're also entering your weight and other profile information — but you can also use the app without entering this information.

Best features

The instructions and built-in workout routines are great for those who are workout novices. Experienced gym rats will appreciate the logging and graphic features, as well as the option to build their own workouts.

Worst features

There's no landscape view (as of this writing), and I'd love to see exercises grouped by skill level.

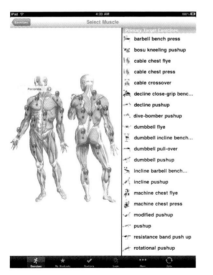 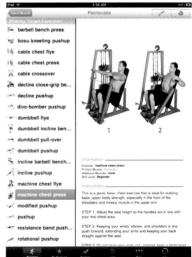

WebMD for iPad
Free

As good as WebMD was when I wrote about it in *Incredible iPhone Apps For Dummies*, it's even better today, especially on the iPad. The larger screen real estate makes searching for medical information even easier.

WebMD for iPad is basically an app-based interface for the information you would find on theWebMD.com Web site. It allows you to look up symptoms and conditions, research drugs, and it offers a lot of First Aid information. The app also now provides a Google Maps–based tool for finding healthcare services, including physicians, hospitals, and pharmacies. In other words, it's a great one-stop shop for a lot of medical information!

So without further ado, let's start with the Home page. Rather than having a navigation bar at the bottom of every page, the app makes its features accessible from the Home page. You'll find buttons for Symptom Checker, Conditions, Drugs & Treatments, First Aid Information, Local Health Listings, and an About tab.

Tap on the Symptoms Checker and you'll get a picture of a naked Ken or Barbie Doll, as you can see in the figure left below, along with a request to enter your profile (Age, Sex, Zip Code). Touch this avatar where you're experiencing symptoms, and you'll get a pop-up window with symptoms pertinent to that specific part of the body. Choose a symptom, answer some questions, and you'll be given some extensive information about what might be causing said symptom, as well as some links to related articles.

The Conditions button will tell you everything you need to know about specific conditions and diseases. For instance, under Influenza, WedMD tells us what it is, what causes it, its symptoms, how it's diagnosed, how it's treated, information about prevention, and a list of frequently asked questions with links to additional articles. There are hundreds of listings here, and you can browse or search through them.

Want to share something in WebMD? Each information page has a button you can tap to e-mail a link to that article on WebMD.com!

One of the most important features in this app is the extensive data-base of prescription drugs. Each drug has information about how it's used and what it is prescribed for, side effects, precautions you should take, interaction issues, and what to do in the case of an overdose (which also includes information about storage and missing a dose). Better yet, many of the drugs include pictures, as you can see in the figure to the right below. If you ever need to identify a drug, this will be important to you. You can even look up drugs by shape, color, or the drug's code, which will be imprinted on it (and on the bottle).

First Aid has a *lot* of information for you with several hundred listings. Most of the listings include treatment details; others tell you, in effect, *Get to a hospital*. Where appropriate, some listings have both home-treatment information and more general information on how medical professionals treat the situation.

Lastly, the Google Maps-powered Listings page will come in handy when you need to find a doctor, hospital, or pharmacy near you.

It's free, and you should get this app.

Best features

The medical information in this app is extensive, and it makes a great resource. The app's layout is professional and easy to navigate, too.

Worst features

What's not to like?

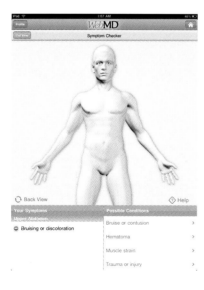

Calorie Tracker — Achieve Your Diet and Fitness Goals — LIVESTRONG.com

$2.99 — Hybrid

This is a companion app for Livestrong.com's The Daily Plate, which is owned by the Lance Armstrong Foundation. You can track your calorie intake and your caloric burn from exercises using the Livestrong. com database of more than 625,000 food and restaurant items, which also includes nutritional information. You don't need an account to use the app, but you can customize a program and regime if you have an account. Your account will also sync with the Web site, your iPhone, and your iPad. This is a hybrid app, so if you bought it for your iPhone after reading our recommendation in *Incredible iPhone Apps For Dummies*, it will work on your iPad, too.

GoMeals HD

Free

Here's another calorie-tracking app, but this one isn't an app interface for an online service. With GoMeals HD, you track your calorie consumption, carbohydrate intake, and how much fat you're eating. The app has a fairly large database of foods, including grocery brands and restaurant brand foods. The app will chart that intake for you in 7-day, 14-day, and 30-day graphs, and break it down by carbs, protein, and fat so you can see at a glance how you're eating. There's also a restaurant finder that allows you to find nearby restaurants. The interface is well designed, though I found it easier to look up foods than to browse for them.

iKamasutra XL — Sex Positions from Kama Sutra and beyond Kamasutra

$2.99

This app is pretty much what you think it is, an app version of *Kama Sutra*, the ancient Indian sex manual with hundreds of sexual positions. It comes complete with illustrations and a description of each position. The app is beautifully designed, the illustrations are not overly graphic, and the descriptions are well written and easy to understand. It has a password mechanism (above and beyond your iPad's passcode) if you need to limit who can open the app, and it allows you to mark positions as Tried, Favorite, or To do. There's even a progress meter that ranks you from Novice to Master.

Navy SEAL Fitness
$1.99 — Hybrid

Come on, you mean I can work out like a Navy SEAL? Okay, *I* couldn't get through a Navy SEAL workout, but maybe you could. This app is based on The Navy SEAL Physical Fitness Guide developed by the U.S. Navy for its elite special forces. Accordingly, it has a lot of information about fitness, exercises, how and why those exercises work, conditioning, and how to work out to achieve the high level of fitness expected of the Navy SEALs. If fitness is your goal, you'll likely appreciate all the research that went into the information in this app.

Zen Timer for iPad — Meditation Timer
$2.99

This app is aimed at people who meditate, whether or not they're specifically practicing Zen meditation. You can use it to time your meditation sessions, mark the starting and ending points with a bell (you can choose from Basu, Dêngzeê, Sakya, Ombu, Kangsê, Zhada, and Shürong bells). You can specify several settings, and then save these as presets. It has a built-in journal and keeps a log and statistics, too. The thing that knocked my socks off, though, is the stunning quality of the bell sounds. They sound absolutely amazing coming out of your iPad's speakers, a touch that will no doubt be appreciated by those who meditate.

9 Music

AmpliTube
Free/$19.99

AmpliTube for iPad is a guitar amp and stomp boxes in an app. If you don't play the guitar, skip ahead to the next item, GrooveMaker Free. AmpliTube is for us guitar geeks.

Think of it as a soundproof practice studio that goes anywhere your iPad goes. Plug in your guitar and earphones and your guitar sounds like you're playing through a huge amp and massive speaker cabinet.

TIP You'll need an adapter like the AmpliTube iRig ($39.99) or GuitarConnect Cable ($29.99) from Griffin Technology. These handy gadgets let you connect both your guitar and your earphones to the iPad, making it possible to jam out using apps like AmpliTube.

The free version comes with one amplifier and speaker cabinet; two microphones — one dynamic and one condenser; and three stomp boxes — Delay, Noise Filter, and Distortion. That's enough to get you started and see if you like playing guitar this way. I know I do.

The free version offers in-app purchase of additional stomp boxes such as Overdrive, Wah, Chorus, Octave, Phazer, and more ($2.99 each) and amp models including Clean Amp, Crunch Amp, and others ($4.99 each). Or buy the paid version and get it all at once for $19.99 — five amp models, five speaker cabinets, 11 stomp-box effects, and more.

Let me mention a couple of nice things AmpliTube does in addition to sounding like a wall of Marshall amps on steroids.

For one it's got a digital tuner, so your guitar never has to be out of tune (unless you want it to be). You can see that my "E" string is perfectly tuned in the figure below.

There's also a metronome, but I rarely use it. Something I use all the time — and love — is the capability to play guitar along with any song in the iTunes Library on my iPad. And I can adjust the volume of the song to hear more or less of my guitar shredding.

And there are 36 presets so you can save all of your favorite guitar setups and recall them with a tap.

The amp, microphone, and stomp box modeling is just terrific. Everything really does sound like its analog counterpart. When you turn the green Overdrive stomp box on, it sounds a lot like playing your guitar through the (green and legendary) Ibanez Tube Screamer, which Overdrive is clearly emulating.

The Fuzz box is nice and fuzzy; the Octave box is surprisingly realistic; the Wah box adds a pleasant wah-wah effect without the bother of a foot pedal.

It's easy to spend a lot of time playing and adjusting the sound of your guitar until it's just right. It sounds so much like real analog amps and stomp boxes that I'm sure you'll have as much fun as I have playing with it.

Best features
Play along with any song and adjust the volume of song or guitar to your taste.

Worst features
No recording whatsoever. I'd like to record my rehearsals, wouldn't you?

GrooveMaker Free
Free

If you fancy yourself a DJ, freestyle rapper, hip-hop producer, or just someone who likes to create dance/hip-hop/rap beats on the fly, GrooveMaker Free is a superb app that lets you do it right on your iPad. Using the app is fun; it's easy; and after you get the hang of it, it's quite addicting.

GrooveMaker Free gives you two free "songs," which in GrooveMaker parlance are remixable groups of audio loops that sound good together.

In the figure below, you can see I've started work on a new project. GrooveMaker gives me eight tracks to play with, and I've filled all eight.

When I tap the Play button near the center of the screen (the one marked Groove), these eight loops begin to play in unison.

If I tap any of the four Mix buttons on the right side of the screen — Random (D), Inst (C), Perc (B), and Mild (A) — GrooveMaker generates a new mix in the chosen genre by changing the loop(s) on one or more of the tracks. Each time I tap any of the mix buttons, I get an entirely new blend of loops.

If I tap the Loops button at the bottom of the screen, the Mix buttons are replaced by a long list of available loops. I can replace the loops on tracks one to eight with different loops.

You can do so much more with this app, but I'm nearly out of space to describe the possibilities. You can adjust the level (volume) and pan (left or right stereo imaging) and Solo or Mute any track. You can save the snippets you build as *grooves*, which you can use as building blocks to create longer *sequences*. Finally, you can export your song as a full-quality 44Khz/16-bit .WAV file to share with friends or burn on a CD.

I've been talking about GrooveMaker Free, but you should know that you can also get almost a dozen different GrooveMaker apps for your iPad including Club, House, Hip-Hop, Techno, Trance, Rock Ace, and Electro. They're available in the App Store as individual standalone apps — or in the free version as in-app purchases; either way, most of them are $9.99. That said, you can still have tons of fun and create unique, great-sounding tracks with only the free version and its two free "songs."

Use the Solo (S) and Mute (M) buttons often. Experiment by adding and removing tracks from the mix until you find just the sound you're looking for.

One last thing: If this kind of app turns you on, check out Looptastic HD ($14.99), an app that's similar to GrooveMaker. It has optional loop sets — Deep House, Latin House, and Club House, to name a few — available for $0.99 each as in-app purchases. But unlike GrooveMaker, Looptastic HD lets you import your own AIFF, WAV, or OGG files as loops.

GrooveMaker is truly a remarkable app with a broad and deep feature set. So I urge you to visit the GrooveMaker Web site (`http://groovemaker.com`) to view the tutorial videos. I guarantee you'll learn some cool tricks that'll help you make better-sounding tracks.

Best features

GrooveMaker has an intuitive user interface and a terrific set of tools. Together they make creating custom musical compositions easy and fun.

Worst features

GrooveMaker doesn't have a way for you to import your own loops.

MultiTrack DAW
$9.99

I've always been fascinated by multi-track recording. I studied audio engineering and began recording music back when multi-track recording meant multimillion-dollar recording gear. I've maintained a home recording studio and have recorded and engineered music pretty much my whole adult life.

That's why MultiTrack DAW (for Digital Audio Workstation), an iPad app that records and mixes up to eight tracks of audio and costs less than ten bucks, blew me away.

What it does is capture really-good-quality audio on up to eight tracks with very little fuss or bother. And I can listen to up to seven tracks I've recorded already while I'm recording on the eighth track, with nary a complaint from my iPad.

You can buy 8 or 16 more stereo tracks (for $7.99 or $15.99, respectively), which is to say the app can play up to 23 individual audio tracks while recording the 24th track.

I couldn't justify the purchase; eight tracks were all *I* needed. The figure on the left below shows me working with those eight tracks. The six buttons are hovering over Track 4 because I pressed-and-held on the recording region in Track 4. They're context-sensitive, too . . . so only buttons that will work appear when you press-and-hold. It's an efficient interface enhancement and I appreciated it.

Anyway, I did what I set out to do — record an entire eight-part song arrangement using nothing but my iPad and Klipsch Image S4i In-Ear Headset with Mic and three-Button Remote ($99).

It worked — but my voice sounded thin and the app offers no on-board effects such as echo, a compressor, an equalizer, or other niceties. That was okay because I wanted to finish the song in GarageBand or Logic on my Mac anyway. MultiTrack DAW has a built-in Wi-Fi server so I just grabbed the tracks for Song2 and dragged them onto the GarageBand or Logic time line.

This was good but I wanted better. I had heard that Apple's iPad Camera Connection Kit will let you use a USB microphone for recording in some apps. It's true — and it worked — so I recorded another eight-track masterpiece using a Blue Yeti, my favorite USB microphone (and what I use for podcasts and voiceovers).

If you are a songwriter, musician, rapper, or poet — or if you love the music of the Four Seasons, Beach Boys, Beatles, and other great vocal acts — MultiTrack DAW is the real deal. You can record and mix up to 24 high-quality audio (44.1kHz, 16-bit; CD-quality) tracks and share them as Linear PCM (.wav), Ogg Audio (.ogg), or MPEG-4 AAC (.aac) files.

I'd be remiss if I didn't mention that there's an app called StudioTrack that almost took this slot. It is another excellent multi-track recorder with excellent outboard effects like compression and EQ. But it can't be upgraded beyond eight tracks. And (inexplicably) there's no input monitor, so you can't hear what you're recording. And worst of all, it's four times the price of MultiTrack DAW at $39.99.

MultiTrack DAW isn't fancy, because it doesn't have to be. It's still a fantastic eight-track recorder at a remarkable price.

Best features

Records and plays back up to eight tracks with no hiccups or other issues. And the clean, simple interface makes it easy to get work done.

Worst features

If I only had a bit of echo, maybe a little compression . . . it lacks effects.

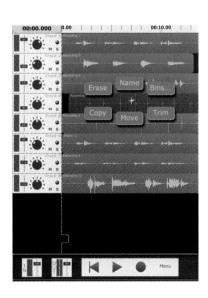

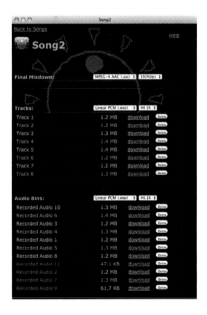

Shazam for iPad
Free

Ever heard a song on the radio or television, in a store, or at a club and wondered what it was called or who was singing it? With the Shazam app, you may never wonder again. Just launch Shazam and point your iPad's microphone at the source of the music. In a few seconds, the song title and artist's name magically appear on your iPad screen, as shown.

Being me, I decided to do my best to stump Shazam. I played wacky selections like *Day Tripper* by Sergio Mendes & Brazil '66, Joe Turner's *Shake, Rattle, and Roll*, *Book of Saturday* from King Crimson's *Larks' Tongues in Aspic*, and even Dinah Washington's *What a Diff'rence a Day Makes*. In more than an hour of testing every obscure song I could find in my iTunes Library, Shazam failed but thrice: *Rockin' Robin* by the Jackson 5, *Hot Venom* by Rebirth Brass Band, and *Justine* by the Cretones. You can see a small fraction of the songs Shazam got right in the figure on the right below.

When Shazam is right, which it almost always is, that song has been *tagged* (in Shazam-speak). Now, if tagging were all Shazam did, that would surely be enough. But wait, there's more: After Shazam tags a song, you can

- ✔ Buy the song at the iTunes store
- ✔ Watch related videos on YouTube
- ✔ Tweet the song on Twitter
- ✔ Read a biography, a discography, or lyrics
- ✔ E-mail a tag to a friend

Okay. I have to admit that Shazam isn't great at identifying classical music, jazz, or opera, but that bothers me not a whit. It's not exactly fantastic with obscure indie bands, though it has gotten better over time. If you use it primarily to identify popular rock music, it rocks.

The iPad version of Shazam is free, with unlimited free tagging, as I write this. But the app's description makes it clear that this is only a "launch offer." So I expect they'll do what they've done with the iPhone versions of Shazam — a free version with five free tags a month and a premium ($4.99) version called Shazam Encore, which offers unlimited tagging and several other exclusive features.

I've tried other apps that claim to do what Shazam does. The best of the bunch for the iPad is SoundHound. It's almost as good as Shazam — and it's a hybrid app, too. That means it works with both iPhone and iPad for the same price ($4.99).

And the iPhone app MusicID with Lyrics is at least as good as Shazam — and probably better — for a lower price ($2.99). And even though it's an iPhone app, it works fine on the iPad in 1x or 2x mode.

But Shazam is king of the heap — at least for as long as it's free with unlimited tagging. If Shazam for iPad ups the price for unlimited tagging, SoundHound or MusicID with Lyrics are both excellent alternatives.

Shazam, SoundHound, and MusicID with Lyrics are all amazing. They work almost everywhere, too — in noisy airport terminals, crowded shopping malls, and even once at a wedding ceremony. Heck, Shazam is so good I gladly coughed up $4.99 for the premium version (Shazam Encore) for my iPhone.

Best features

Can name most contemporary songs and artists in 30 seconds or less.

Worst features

Song lyrics are only available sporadically.

Aphonium SE and Aphonium
$2.99/$5.99

Is Aphonium a generative artwork? A playable musical instrument? A soothing meditation aid or beautiful timepiece? Aphonium is all these things, yet so much more.

That is straight from the App Store description of Aphonium because you'd never buy it if *I* said it. Strange as it sounds (ha!), Aphonium really *is* all those things and more.

Aphonium has three different "scenes," as its modes are called. The Immerse scene lets you and gravity interact with shapes that move around on the screen. The Compose scene, shown in the figure below, draws shapes and plays instruments when you tap. And the Conduct scene lets you control what you see and hear by dragging or tapping.

In the top-left corner are five icons: The musical note icon opens the scenes menu as shown below. The smiley face opens the moods menu, which contains combinations of instruments, shapes, and colors that together make a "mood." The clock icon enables and disables the date and time display (in the middle of the screen). The crescent-moon icon is a sleep timer. And the gear icon opens the settings menu.

To enjoy Aphonium, put on your earphones, pick a scene and a mood, and start tapping on and dragging your finger around the screen. In a nutshell, Aphonium generates beautiful animated graphics that match the music generated by either the app's artificial-intelligence engine or your fingers on the touch screen.

Now play around with all three scenes and 17 moods until you get the hang of it. My favorite scene is Compose with the grid lines and instrument names turned on (the icon with three vertical lines, at bottom-right in the figure below) and Evolve When Idle (little child and adult icon with a green dot that indicates it's enabled) turned on. I tap a few times to get it started, and then I can sit back and enjoy mostly decent sound and always interesting animation generated by the program in real time.

You'll either love the Evolve When Idle setting or you won't. When enabled, it makes your iPad continue to act like you're tapping and dragging on its screen, even if you're not touching the screen. It continues to create original "music" and art until you change scenes, shake your iPad three times to clear the screen, or quit the app.

Aphonium SE costs $2.99, and the other version — known as plain-old "Aphonium" — costs $5.99. What does the additional $3.00 buy you? Glad you asked. You know those 17 moods I mentioned before? In Aphonium SE that's all you get. In the premium edition, you get those 17 to start with — and can also create your own moods, choosing from a plethora of musical instruments, ambient sounds, and a variety of shapes and colors.

Buy Aphonium SE for $2.99. It's worth it. Then, if you like it as much as I do, you'll want to upgrade to the premium version for $5.99 and unlock the limitless potential of creating and editing moods.

Best features

It has a great sound library with dozens of great-sounding instruments and interesting ambient sounds. And just when you think you've seen every possible shape, a new shape appears.

Worst features

Some instruments are too quiet, even on the loudest setting, and some instruments are much louder than others — so it can be hard to get just the right blend of tones.

Songwriter's Pad
$9.99

If you're a songwriter, wanna-be songwriter, poet, or wanna-be poet, Songwriter's Pad is a great tool for writing songs and poems on your iPad. The rhyming dictionary is good. Choosing words and phrases delineated in emotional categories such as love, hate, happy, anger, and fear, can feel kind of sappy. And some of the phrases supplied to fire your imagination may tickle your funny bone instead. But . . . if phrases like "you ripped my heart out" and "you must be off your rocker" get your creative juices flowing, just wait until you check out the way-cool rhyming dictionary and thesaurus.

Bebot — Robot Synth
$1.99 US

Bebot is a clever app that's part robot and part polyphonic musical synthesizer. When you touch the screen, the robot moves and makes different sounds controlled by your finger movements. With four-finger multitouch polyphony, multiple synthesis modes, user-definable presets and scales, adjustable synth settings and effects — and more — Bebot is sophisticated but still simple enough for anyone to use and enjoy.

If you're a fan of the Beach Boys, select the Theremin preset and see if you can re-create the theremin part in "Good Vibrations." (Don't know what a theremin is? Look it up. Don't know what it sounds like? It's the unearthly sound in the choruses and at the end of "Good Vibrations.")

ImproVox
$7.99

ImproVox refers to itself as "a new vocal instrument," and that's an apt description. As you sing you move your fingers on the two touch pads on the screen. One touchpad corrects the pitch of your voice (à la AutoTune) while it generates real-time four-part harmonies in five styles — choral, pop, barbershop, jazz, and baroque. The second touchpad governs vocal effects like reverb, echo, flanger, and auto-wah.

If you've ever wanted to create that doo-wop sound but lacked the talent to sing vocal harmonies with yourself, ImproVox provides hours and hours of great-sounding entertainment.

It's so cool I never wanted to stop.

Pandora Radio
Free

Pandora Radio is one of the coolest concepts ever. You tell it the names of your favorite musicians and songs, and then Pandora creates an instant personalized radio station that plays only songs that exemplify the style of music represented by the artists and songs you named.

I based one of my Pandora stations on songs by the Byrds, Tom Petty, and the Beatles. The result is a station with songs by those artists — but also a lot of similar music by artists with whom I'm not familiar. I made another station based on music by Dave Brubeck that plays great music by jazz artists I've never heard before.

Pandora Radio is free. It's awesome. Give it a try.

This Day in Music
$2.99

If you love music, you'll love This Day in Music, an app chock-full of music trivia and facts. Look back in time to discover important events from the music world that took place on this date. Who was born? Who died? Who had a first hit single? There's a multiple-choice music quiz, music trivia and facts, and you can discover which stars share your birthday and what song was Number 1 on the day you were born.

10 News & Information

BBC News
Free (Ad-Supported) — Hybrid

 I loves me some BBC. I personally think it is one of the top news organizations in the world, and BBC News brings it all to my iPad (and iPhone)! The BBC organization generates written news, broadcast news, and one of the most-listened-to radio news programs on the planet (it's broadcast all over the world, after all), and the BBC News app offers this content to us in a user-friendly way that makes it a pleasure to use.

Let's start with the home page. When you launch BBC News, it will take a couple of moments to download all the recent content that's displayed. That content is presented in several different categories, including Top Stories, Americas, Technology, and so on, each with its own row of scrollable boxes that represents an individual story. Just swipe from left to right to see more headlines, along with accompanying pictures. Tap a box, and the story is presented on the right, as you can see in the figure below (in portrait view, you get one category row at the top of the screen, which is similar to the iPhone's view). Swipe vertically to scroll through longer articles; there's also a Sharing button that allows you to post the current article to Facebook and Twitter, or to e-mail it to someone.

Just about every story has an accompanying photograph or illustration, but some articles, like the one in the figure below, have accompanying video reports instead. Tap them and a video player takes over the screen, nice and easy. Some of these videos are broadcast TV news reports; some are interviews and other kinds of supporting video that add depth to the story, should you choose to watch it.

 If you're using a wireless plan to access the Internet on your iPad, be sure you don't go over your data caps when watching videos!

Back on the home page, you can swipe up and down in the headline lists to see more categories of stories. Only a few of the categories are expanded to show their article boxes automatically by default. The rest are collapsed; if you tap one, it opens out, just like the categories featured at the top. You can edit this list, too, deciding which categories are featured (thus automatically expanded) and which are not.

Another great feature is the Live Radio button in the top-left corner of the screen. Tap this any time and you get a live stream of current BBC News programming, which I love. I very much respect the BBC's reporting, and having the BBC News stream a mere tap away makes it easy for me to tune in to any time.

Best features

Awesome BBC News content, delivered in an easy-to-use format — plus a live radio stream — add up to a great app.

Worst features

I'd like to be able to listen to archived news shows and other radio magazines, rather than just the live stream.

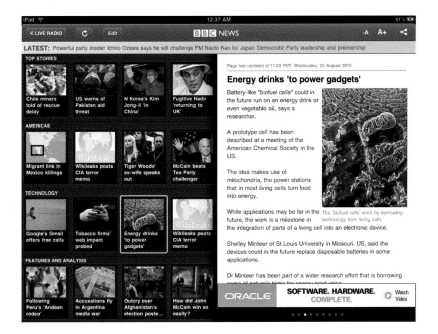

Flipboard
Free

Honestly, I don't know how I feel personally about Flipboard just yet. Oh, it's a very cool app, which is why it's being included in this book, but this is one of those apps — kind of like Pulse (which I review below) — that polarizes people. It's also one of the most heavily reviewed iPad apps I've yet seen, with four- and five-star reviews almost perfectly balanced by one-star reviews and a right-down-the-middle three-star average. That's often a sign that someone did something right, so let's look at what's so different about this app!

Flipboard builds itself as a social magazine. It's part RSS news reader and partly a new way to view social-networking content, a lot of which is news linked to by our friends. The flagship feature of this Flipboard is to turn your RSS feeds — including your Facebook Wall and Twitter feed — into a magazine-like spread. No, seriously. In Twitter, for instance, the app takes recent posts from those you follow and lays them out like magazine articles, as you can see in the figure to the left below.

If the tweet includes a link to a photo, that photo is incorporated into the layout. If it links to a news article or other Web page, elements from that article are included — with a link to the full Web page, which you can view through the in-app browser. In addition, only the Tweeter's name from these links to articles is included in Flipboard, not the original text (tweets that are just text are shown verbatim). That certainly represents a different way to look at your Twitter feed.

Facebook is very similar — posts from your friends are laid out like magazine articles, but now we also get all kinds of status updates like songs people are listening to (Flipboard grabs the album-cover art for the song), and videos that are linked to can be played directly in the app. In the figure to the right below, you'll see an album cover, a comment about the touring version of *Jersey Boys*, and links to two articles posted by some friends of mine.

Once you've entered your Facebook and Twitter information, don't be surprised if (next time you launch the app) you see the face of one of your cousins panning across your iPad's screen as if he'd been featured on the cover of a magazine! It was pretty surreal the first time I saw that.

Of course, Flipboard also supports some straight RSS news feeds, though this is limited to a list of less than a hundred feeds as of this writing, with more coming. Those feeds include a variety of commercial magazines, blogs, major media outlets, and individual RSS feeds of some famous people. There're also several customized feeds for news, photos, and such, developed by the company for use in the app. There's one more limitation I should mention, and that's the current cap of only nine feeds (a curious limitation, to be sure).

All in all, Flipboard is a very interesting app, and I look forward to seeing how it evolves in the future.

Best features

Flipboard can make even the most mundane content look sexy, or at least interesting and professional!

Worst features

I want to be able to add my own RSS feeds, and I also want to have more than nine feeds.

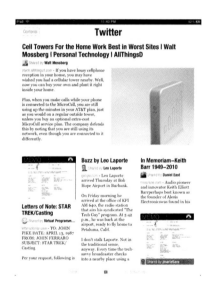

NPR for iPad
Free

This is another one of those apps that makes the iPad a real pleasure to use. First of all, it offers direct access to almost everything National Public Radio has to offer, from cultural articles, to game shows, to NPR's world-class news. Better yet, it has a great layout, the kind of layout you only get when the developers truly grok the iPad.

NPR for iPad offers up its content in several ways. Current stories are provided on the home screen of the app in three scrollable time lines — one each for News, Arts & Life, and Music — as you can see in the figure to the left below. These are all stories from NPR the news organization — the different radio programs are offered separately. You can swipe through these three streams from left to right, and when you tap a story that interests you, it takes over the screen, with the category stream at the bottom, which you can see in the figure to the right below.

If you see a picture in a story that interests you, tap it for a full-screen version.

The articles in these three streams are a mix of text-based articles and stories that also have an audio report, as you would expect from National Public *Radio*. You can listen to the audio report immediately by tapping the Listen Now buttons, or drop it into a Playlist for later listening. A nice touch in the app is that you can continue to browse the app when something is playing. In the figure to the right below, I am listening to a segment from *Wait, Wait . . . Don't Tell Me!* while I read a news article.

Don't worry if you're listening to something and have to leave the app. When you open it again, your Playlist is still there — and you're asked whether you want to resume listening where you left off!

You can also browse NPR's radio content by program. Not every show is represented (Where's *Says You!?*), and not every program has full episodes, but most do; if you have a favorite NPR show you otherwise find difficult to follow, you'll appreciate this feature.

Another great feature is the capability to stream local stations. Public Radio fans often grow attached to a particular station, and this app makes it easy to follow your favorite. You can also look for a particular show being streamed somewhere, and pick a station that way. Either way, it makes it easy for you to support individual stations.

Lastly, there's a quick button on the Home screen that lets you listen to the current top-of-the-hour news that NPR News updates.

 You do get some advertising with this app, in the form of an occasional (short) full-screen interstitial and a sponsor badge on the Home screen. It's a small price to pay for all that otherwise-free content.

NPR for iPad is a great app for people who have missed part or all of a story or program on the radio — and for those who simply want to manage their NPR content when and where they want.

Best features

A great layout makes this app a pleasure to use, and the content is second to none.

Worst features

I wish I could access every single NPR show, and that all those shows provided full episodes, but what's there is great.

Pulse News
$3.99

As far as I can tell, there are two kinds of RSS fans in the world, those who love Pulse and those who hate it. Count me among those who love it. Alphhonso Labs took the idea of a "News Reader" in an entirely new direction and made it look sexy, as you can see in the figure to the left below.

If that figure doesn't strike you as "sexy," you can probably count yourself in that other camp — you know, the ones who hate Pulse.

The key to Pulse is its main view, which is again in the figure to the left below. There are four rows of squares — each row represents a different RSS feed, and each square represents a different article in that feed, including any images. You swipe horizontally to browse through all your feeds, and you swipe vertically to browse through an individual feed. It's slick, simple, and visually appealing, especially if your RSS feeds use attractive images.

When you tap any particular article, all the other feeds disappear and the full RSS listing takes over the rest of the page, as you can see in the figure to the right below. Pulse's presentation makes for a very clean page. If you want to read more, you can tap the headline or the Web button at the top-right of the screen. That activates the built-in browser, which pulls up the Web-based version of the full article. I tell you, it's simple, and it makes for some pleasant viewing.

I used portrait mode for my screenshots because that was the only way to show you two of them, but this app looks best in landscape mode. In fact, the developers talk about how they designed it for "two thumbs" mode because that's how they saw people using their iPads in coffee shops!

Another great feature of Pulse is the way you manage your RSS feeds. You can enter the URL directly for any RSS feed if you know it (or if you've it copied to your clipboard), but you can also do a search — say, for "The Mac Observer" (that's a great thing to search for!). When you do so, Pulse taps into Google and returns results pertaining to your search, but it only shows results with actual RSS feeds. Then all you have to do is tap the one you want and it's added to Pulse!

There's one more feature I have time to mention: If you tap the heart icon when looking at any given article, you can either save what you're reading for later or use it to create your own Pulse. A Pulse is your own RSS feed that other people can follow, and it's made up entirely of articles you choose.

The only downside of this app, in my opinion, is that it supports only 20 feeds, plus five additional Pulses (the developers say they're working on adding more). That makes it a great reader for casual RSS users, but if you have 30, 50, 100, or more feeds you (somehow find time to) follow, you'll want to look at one of the other news readers in this chapter.

Best features

This app has two great features: The home page view and the capability to add RSS feeds by search.

Worst features

20 RSS feeds just isn't enough!

WIRED Magazine
Free (Each issue is $3.99)

It didn't come as much of a surprise to me that *Wired* magazine understood how to make a print magazine into a compelling digital offering, but even with heightened expectations I was impressed with this app. *Wired* has always been one of the best-looking magazines around, but on the iPad, it's interactive too!

To start with, the app is a free download, but don't let that fool you. Think of the app as a shell for multiple issues of the magazine. The app is free, but to get each issue, you have to make an in-app purchase. Fortunately, the publishers put together an iPad-only issue called iPad Edition Free Preview so you can check it out. Offering it was a smart move on *Wired*'s part. The review has just a few articles, but the full issues have all the content of their printed siblings — indeed, more, because each iPad issue has exclusive iPad articles!

Another exclusive feature for the iPad version (at least until *Wired* goes to Android) are in-article videos. Try that in a print magazine! Just tap one of these videos that include bonus content and it opens up in a full-screen player. In addition to the occasional video, some images are interactive too. How cool is that?

When you download your first issue, the first thing you're likely to notice is that the cover is tappable. That's right — if a headline grabs your attention, just tap it to go straight to that article! How many times have you flipped back and forth in a magazine looking for some article featured on the cover but seemingly hidden within? No more!

The other thing to learn about navigating is that articles longer than one page scroll vertically, with a swipe. To get from article to article, you swipe horizontally. The cool thing is that you can swipe to the next article from anywhere in your current article. The app's makers don't force you to go to the beginning or end or some such.

You can also navigate by tapping once to get a navigation pane up top and a scrolling slider at the bottom. Use that slider to jump to any page you want. Tap the table of contents icon on top and you get a list of articles; if you tap the graph bars to the right, you'll see articles laid out with all of their pages, as you can see in the figure to the right below. That's super cool!

One last note: Some people may be put off at the full-page advertising in each issue, but the economic reality is that even with no printing costs, it takes advertising and a modest newsstand price to pay for professional content. Besides, magazines are one medium where people routinely want to look at a lot of the ads. In other words, accept it as the cost of getting this gorgeous content to your iPad.

Best features

I love the movies, and I love that I can swipe sideways to another article, no matter where I am in long, multi-page articles. I also love the thumbnail slider for visually navigating the app.

Worst features

We should be able to subscribe for a discounted price. Everyone would win with subscriptions, but there are a lot of fingers in the pie (including Apple's) that make such things not as straightforward as you might think.

Blogshelf
$2.99 — Hybrid

Here's another approach for an RSS news reader: Blogshelf presents RSS feeds as if they were magazines on a bookshelf, somewhat similar to (if less pretty than) Apple's iBooks. Tap a feed and you'll get current articles presented in a nice, clean list form. Tap through to an article, and just the RSS content is offered. Tap through on the title, and you're taken to the article's full Web page in the in-app browser. You can mark favorites, e-mail or tweet an article, or swipe through to the next article. Casual RSS users looking for a low-key way to read their feeds might find this reader to their liking.

Reeder for iPad
$4.99

If you use Google Reader — the search giant's free RSS news feed service — you'll want this app. You can use it to browse your Google Reader news feeds by feed or by folder, manage starred items, and share stories through e-mail and Twitter. The app supports Instapaper, ReadItLater, Delicious (also known as del.icio.us), and Pinbard, and you can open articles directly in Safari. It uses a binder metaphor for browsing through your RSS feeds; all your controls are conveniently lined up on the left. About the only thing you can't do with it is add new feeds to your account, but every Google Reader user I know swears by this app.

USA Today for iPad
Free

USA Today is the national daily published by Gannett Company, and it was among the first newspapers to embrace the iPad. Navigation is good (tap the *USA Today* logo for quick section navigation), the layout is nice, and you get national and local news, sports scores, local weather, lots of photos, including a gallery of the day's best photos (tap the photo to get the caption), and the option to participate in a daily poll called The USA Today Snapshot. Lastly, you can share articles via e-mail, Twitter, and Facebook. This app is slick, well designed, and it looks great!

Wall Street Journal

Free (but subscription required)

The Wall Street Journal is one of the world's foremost business newspapers, and its parent company, News Corp., is at the forefront of developing new business models for today's publishing marketplace. Accordingly, the pricing schemes for this app have shifted precipitously, but as of this writing it's free with an online subscription to the paper. Be that as it may, the *Journal*'s iPad app is a must-have if you want to follow the newspaper on your iOS device. Navigation is simple, and it looks great, too.

Zinio Magazine Newsstand & Reader

Free

Zinio is another big outlet for magazines, and it also serves as a shell for multiple issues of each of those magazines. In fact, it's more like iBooks than the Wired app, because you can buy multiple magazines within the app. That said, therein lies a downside in the app: Not every digital edition of every magazine is a stellar example of great iPad design. Still, there are a lot of magazines published under the Zinio umbrella, and if you want to read them on your iPad, Zinio makes it possible.

11 Productivity

Corkulous
$3.99

The App Store description of Corkulous calls it an *idea board* that provides a way to collect, organize, and share your ideas in a way that feels completely natural. Naturally, I agree completely.

As you might expect from its moniker, Corkulous uses a corkboard as its metaphor. You start with a single corkboard but can then create as many additional corkboards as you like.

You can password-protect any or all of your corkboards, a nice touch.

At the bottom of each corkboard is a pop-out file drawer that contains your tools, as shown in the figure on the left below. From left to right those tools are Labels, Notes, Tasks, Contacts, Photos, and Boards.

Label and Task items are single-line items for jotting down short notes or things you need to do. Both offer you a choice of four different typefaces (fonts), in sizes ranging from tiny to huge. The major difference between a Label and a Task is that a Task includes a check box that dims the text when you tap the Task to check it off, as shown in the "Send Lisa flowers" Task in the figure on the left below.

Notes can be as long or short as you like. And (since Notes are digital knock-offs of those ubiquitous 3M Post-It™ Notes) you have a choice of colors, as shown in the figure on the right below. And Notes give you a choice of left-, center-, or right-justification in addition to four typefaces and unlimited text sizes.

Contacts, such as Lisa and Kyle in the figures below, represent people in your iPad's Contacts app. If you double-tap a Contact, all the info for that contact appears in a floating overlay, which you can edit or copy at will.

Photos let you choose a picture from your iPad's Photos app and place a resizable copy anywhere on a corkboard.

Finally, Boards let you create sub-corkboards, so you never run out of space, no matter how many items you create.

What I like best is that every element worked as I expected it to work. For example, you pinch and un-pinch to zoom in and out; you tap and drag an individual item to move it to a new location; you tap on the corkboard and drag out a selection rectangle to select multiple items; you double-tap an item to edit it; and you press and hold on an item to cut or copy it.

Finally, you can export all or part of any corkboard:

- ✔ To an e-mail message
- ✔ To the iTunes File Sharing section
- ✔ To Your iPad's Photos app
- ✔ With or without the cork background
- ✔ As a PDF or a JPG file

If you're not convinced yet, go watch the demo video at `http://www.appigo.com`.

Best features

It's drop-dead simple to use and has virtually no learning curve.

Worst features

You can't create any kind of graphic element — no lines, arrows, circles, squares, or any such thing.

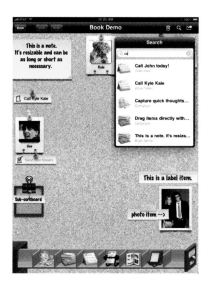
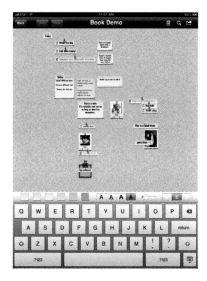

Dropbox
Free

This could get confusing. You see, Dropbox is not only the name of this iPad app, it's also the name of the company, the name of the service it provides, and the name of the software that runs on your iPhone or Mac, Windows, and Linux computers. So I'll call the iPad version *Dropbox iPad app,* and refer to the other parts as plain ol' *Dropbox.*

I was a huge fan of Dropbox (www.dropbox.com) long before the Dropbox iPad app came along. To understand the beauty of the Dropbox iPad app, you first need to know what Dropbox is and how it works.

Dropbox is, in a nutshell, software that synchs your files online and across your computers. You can use it to synchronize files among as many Mac, Windows, or Linux computers as you want. You can use it to share files with anyone you want. And you can use it to back up important documents.

You first create a free Dropbox account and install the free Dropbox software on your computers (let's call them Computer 1 and Computer 2). A folder named (what else) Dropbox appears on each computer; all files you put in the Dropbox folder on Computer 1 are instantly available in the Dropbox folder on Computer 2, and vice versa. Plus, because Dropbox stores those files on its own secure servers, you can access them from anywhere with any Web browser.

Whew. Now that you know how the Dropbox system works, I can tell you about the Dropbox iPad app, which gives you access to files in your Dropbox folder(s) from your iPad.

With the Dropbox iPad app, you can use the Internet connection on your iPad to view the files in your computer's Dropbox folder, as shown in the figure on the left. You can also specify "favorite" files that are automatically copied to your iPad so you can access them without an Internet connection, and you can e-mail links to the files in your Dropbox so your friends can download them.

Wondering what kinds of files you can view in the Dropbox app? Well, you can view all the usual suspects: Microsoft Office (Word, Excel, and PowerPoint) files; Apple iWork (Pages, Numbers, and Keynote) files; .PDF files; most types of image files such as (but not limited to) .JPEG, .TIFF, and .PNG; as well as music and video files. You can also upload photos or movies from your iPhone to your Dropbox folder.

You can save image files to the Photos library where they're available for editing by photo-editing apps like the ones I described in Chapter 1 — Photogene, Strip Designer, Color Splash, and the like — and you can open other document types with certain other iPad apps. For example, if you want to edit a Microsoft Word .DOC file that's in your Dropbox folder, you'll be offered a choice of apps that can edit a .DOC file. Such apps include Pages, (covered in Chapter 3), and Print n Share or GoodReader (covered in this chapter).

I love Dropbox. Let me tell you a couple of ways I use it:

✔ I use it for current projects so I have access to those files from any computer in the world, as well as from my iPad and iPhone. Because the files are both saved on my hard disk and stored on the secure Dropbox server, they serve as an up-to-the-minute backup of my files.

✔ Whenever I travel, I put my best photos in a shared Dropbox folder so my friends and family can enjoy them at their convenience.

Best features

Free app with 2GB of free online storage that you can use any way you like.

Worst features

Unlike Dropbox on a computer, the iPad app won't let you share links to folders — you can only share links to individual files.

OmniGraffle
$49.99

I'm a visual thinker, and one of my favorite ways to brainstorm is to use a flow-charting or mind-mapping program such as OmniGraffle for the Mac, Visio for Windows, or Inspiration on either platform.

OmniGraffle for the iPad is the best thing I've found for creating flow-charts and mind maps on my iPad. It combines the best of all three of the aforementioned programs and delivers them on the iPad's touch screen — via what is possibly the best user interface of any iPad app. Read that again — I said *any* iPad app. I wish most of the other iPad apps I use regularly were as thoughtfully designed, powerful, and easy to use as OmniGraffle.

What I like best about OmniGraffle is the way it uses Stencils. *Stencils* are collections of pre-made shapes, images, and connectors to use in your documents, as shown in the figure on the left below. On the right side of this image you see the set of Stencil libraries that come with OmniGraffle; they include Connections, Shapes, Software, Three-Dimensional, and several others. I've since added a bunch of third-party stencil sets for other uses — such as Web flowcharts, home-theater connections, video lighting, camera staging, and more.

Using Stencil objects is a pleasure. Drag an item from a Stencil collection onto the canvas and the object behaves just as you expect an object to behave — just as objects behave in your favorite desktop graphics applications such as Photoshop, Illustrator, InDesign, and so on. Tap an object to select it or tap and drag to select multiple objects at once. Selected items have "handles" on the corners and sides, just as you'd expect.

Another powerful tool is the Contents popover, which lets you

✔ Select an object or multiple objects according to their style, as shown on the left side of the image on the left below ("Select objects by style")

✔ Change the stacking order of objects

✔ Create and manage layers as shown on the left side of the image on the right below ("Canvas 1")

✔ Create and manage multiple canvases in the same document

And (of course) it's easy to modify any object so it looks just the way you like. Select the object and then tap the little "i" in the menu bar. A full-featured inspector, which says "Info" on the right side of the figure on the right below, lets you modify any attribute with just a couple of taps.

Stencils and objects are merely the tip of the iceberg. You can also draw freehand shapes right onto the canvas as shown in the figure on the right below. The stars, arrows, and cartoon bubble are Stencil objects, but everything else is drawn freehand.

Intelligent diagramming is another OmniGraffle strength, making it simple to create organization charts, flowcharts, and other structured documents that require shapes and lines to remain connected when they're moved.

And you've got to love *smart guides*, which make it easy to align and distribute objects. When you move a shape, a marker will indicate when it forms an equally spaced row or column, or when it's aligned with the left, right, top, bottom, or center of another object. When you rotate or resize an object, a marker lets you know when your rotation or size matches other objects on the canvas.

Best features

OmniGraffle offers one of the most phenomenal user interfaces I've ever used on my iPad. If only all productivity apps were this well designed.

Worst features

At $49.99, it's one of the most expensive productivity apps available today. On the other hand, its supremely usable interface and superb feature set make it worth that much and more. If you're too cheap to pop for it, check out apps like Whiteboard HD ($5.99), Instaviz ($9.99), or even OmniGraphSketcher ($14.99; covered in Chapter 3). They're not the same but they may suit your needs.

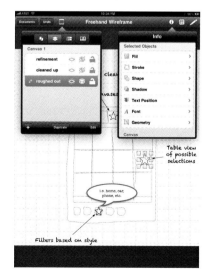

Print n Share
$8.99 US

If you ever have to print documents on your Mac or PC — whether locally over your Wi-Fi network or remotely over 3G or EDGE — Print n Share is what you need. Plus, it's so chock-full of other useful features that I hardly know where to start.

Let's start with the basics. If you have a Wi-Fi-enabled printer, setting up printing couldn't be easier. I launched Print n Share on my iPad and it immediately discovered both Wi-Fi printers in my house. I could print to both within a few seconds of launching the app for the first time.

The app understands lots of common file types, including .doc, .docx, .xls, .xlsx, .txt, .html, .PDF, Pages, Numbers, and many other file types, some of which are shown in the image on the left below. So not only can you print them from your iPad, you can also preview them before you commit to printing. You can even edit text files right in Print n Share before printing them.

Print n Share includes a built-in Wi-Fi solid-state drive that lets you drag and drop files between your iPad and your computer, so you don't have to waste time connecting via USB and performing a sync.

Using this app, you can also zip and unzip files right on your iPad, which means archived zip files present no problem whatsoever. Not many iPad apps can deal with zipped files; this capability has saved my bacon more than once.

If that were all it could do, I'd recommend it wholeheartedly. But it does much more. For example, there's a full-featured e-mail client built into Print n Share; you can send and receive mail, print messages and enclosures, and save messages and enclosures as files on your iPad. Did I mention that it works with as many e-mail accounts as you like? Or that it also has its own multi-language spell checker with word suggestions? Heck, it even has features that aren't available in the Mail app that came with your iPad — such as a unified inbox for all mail accounts and the capability to create multiple signatures with images and formatted text!

By the time you read this, your iPad may be running iOS 4. One of the most ballyhooed features of iOS 4 is its unified inbox for all of your e-mail accounts. (If your iPad already has a unified inbox, I'm glad to be wrong just now.)

But I'm not even close to finished yet. Print n Share also includes a built-in Web browser so you can print, save, or e-mail Web pages and import bookmarks from your Mac or PC, as shown in the figure on the right. You can print contacts from your Contacts app in several formats, including mailing labels. And you have myriad options for printing photos from your Photos app.

Finally, I've had several *Incredible iPhone Apps For Dummies* readers mention that EuroSmartz (the creator of Print n Share) provides fast, excellent technical support.

I've tried several apps that purport to allow printing from your iPad; Print n Share is the only one that was easy to set up and worked reliably. In my humble opinion, it's the only way to go if you need a dependable app for printing documents from your iPad.

There is one last thing: Just as this book was going to press Apple announced that the next release of the iPad Operating System, iOS 4.2, will include its own printing facility. That said, I doubt Apple's solution will be as comprehensive and will have fewer bells and whistles.

Best features

Print n Share offers a variety of ways to access documents on your iPad and print them on a remote printer. It's easy to set up, easy to use, and reliable.

Worst features

I'm not sure this is a bad thing but Print n Share has so many features that it's easy to forget to use some of them.

Things
$19.99

I've moved my to-do items and projects among nearly a dozen iPad apps for so long that I now know them by heart. I've tried apps that are more expensive, less expensive, ad-supported, and free, but at the end of the day the one I liked best was Cultured Code's Things.

Don't get me wrong — there's no shortage of excellent apps out there to help you manage tasks and projects; selecting Things over all the others was perhaps the toughest choice I made for this chapter (or even this whole book). And since managing your tasks and projects is such a personal thing, you might prefer one of the other apps such as OmniFocus, Todo, TaskPaper, or Toodledo, all of which came very close to occupying this space in the book.

But, at the end of the day (actually, at the end of several months), it was Things I continued to use — and here's why:

- ✔ Unlike some other task-management apps, Things for the iPad was easy to set up and use. I understood most of its features and how to use them within minutes — without reading a word. I suppose it's a testament to the user interface that there's no online help or manual (though the Things Web site has some tips and hints).

- ✔ I'm a big fan of David Allen's Getting Things Done (GTD) work-life management system (www.davidco.com), though I'm not a strict adherent and prefer a loose interpretation of its steps. Unlike some other apps, Things easily adapted to my style — while (at the same time) offering pretty much a full implementation of GTD if you want it. Some apps force most or all of the GTD methodologies on you, and in the process make it more difficult to use the app the way you want.

In Things, you get to choose which elements you like to use. If you don't care about projects and only want to manage tasks and to do items on the list, that's fine. But if you have multi-stage projects with varying deadlines and components, Things can handle those just as easily. Do you like to use Tags to further delineate your tasks? They're in there if you want them but unobtrusive if you don't. Do you organize your tasks by Areas of Responsibility? (Do you even know what that means? It doesn't matter.) Like Tags, Areas of Responsibility are available if you want them and invisible if you don't.

Finally, Things's user interface is remarkable — it's simple, clean, and uncluttered, as you see in the image below. My hat is off to the developers and designers of Things, for packing so much flexibility and power into such a simple, easy-to-use interface.

Actually, there is one more last thing, but it only matters if you use a Mac: Using the Mac version of Things in tandem with the iPad version is blissful. Synchronization is easy to set up and automatic once you do. Plus, there's also an iPhone version of Things, so you can keep all three — Mac, iPad, and iPhone — on the same proverbial page.

Best features

Things's simple yet powerful user interface is surely its finest feature. Even things you can't see in the image below, such as data entry and searching or reorganizing items, are powerful yet easy to use.

Worst features

If you're using a Windows PC, there's no Windows version of Things. And although the developer has indicated that you'll soon be able to synch the iPhone and iPad versions with each other, you can't currently do so without the Mac version in the middle. And finally, I think it's kind of cheesy to sell separate versions for the iPhone and the iPad, especially if you charge more for the iPad version. The iPhone version is $9.99 while the iPad version is $19.99. It makes me feel warm and fuzzy about other developers, the ones who create hybrid versions of their apps for one reasonable price.

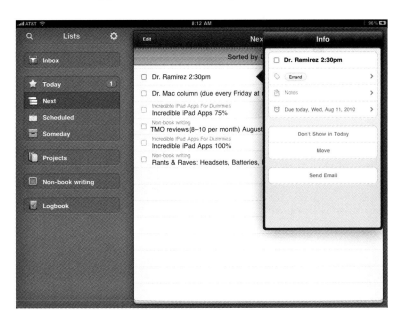

Dragon Dictation
Free

Wouldn't it be nice if, instead of having to type text or e-mail messages, you could dictate them and have your spoken words magically translated into text? If that sounds good to you, you'll love Dragon Dictation. Just tap the big red Tap and Dictate button and speak into your iPad's microphone. Tap anywhere on the screen when you're done talking and in a few seconds, the words you just spoke appear onscreen as text. Then just tap to cut or copy the text, send it as an e-mail message, or post it as a Facebook or Twitter status update.

In a word (actually three), Dragon Dictation rocks!

GoodReader
$0.99

GoodReader is one of those apps you won't know you need until you actually need it. Its specialty is letting you read the huge PDF or text files that bring other iPad apps to their knees. It's also one of the best apps for reading just about anything — including Microsoft Word, PowerPoint, and Excel files; iWork '08 and '09 files; Web pages and Safari webarchive files, plus a number of high-resolution image-file formats. With bookmarks, search, full-screen reading mode, and easy importing from iTunes, iDisk, Dropbox, and other sources, GoodReader is one of the most-used apps on my iPad.

Instapaper
$4.99

Have you ever happened upon a Web page with a long, interesting story you wanted to read but don't have time? Or have you wished you could somehow stick the story in your pocket and read it during the train ride home, on the airplane, or during some other downtime? If you've ever wished those things, you're going to love Instapaper — an iPad app that lets you save Web pages from any browser and read them later on your iPad, with or without an Internet connection.

Give the tilt-to-scroll option a chance. I hated it at first but now think it should be in every iPad app.

SoundNote
$4.99

Microsoft Word for the Mac and Microsoft OneNote for Windows both offer a feature I consider essential to my work: They let you record audio while you type notes — and the notes are then synchronized with the recording. So, for example, if Steve Jobs says, "We've sold three million iPads in the first 80 days," I type something like, "3 mil in 80 days." When I write the story, I just click next to the words, "3 mil in 80 days" and listen to the audio from that particular portion of the speech.

I tested several iPad apps with this feature and SoundNote was, hands down, the best of the bunch.

 ## Use Your Handwriting
Free

 Yes, Use Your Handwriting is yet another to-do list organizer/reminder type app, but it has a unique twist: You can't type notes or even speak them. Instead, as the app's name implies, when you use Use Your Handwriting, you write your notes by hand (actually by finger). I love the way the screen scrolls automatically to allow you to write entire sentences on one line.

12 Reference

Manual for the United States of America
$1.99 — Hybrid

Have you ever wondered who signed the Declaration of Independence? Yeah, we all know Thomas Jefferson, Ben Franklin, and that most famous of signatures, John Hancock — but how about Caesar Rodney and Josiah Bartlett? Well, there's an app for that! Manual for the United States of America has this kind of information, and a lot more about this country and its government, too.

Let's go back to the Declaration of Independence. You'll find the full text of the document — as you can see in the figure to the left below — a scan of one of the original copies, an image of an engraving of the document, and that list of all the signers. Better yet is the fact that there is an image and short biography of every signer. Those bios are mostly lists of political offices the signers held throughout their lives. I personally knew next to nothing about most of these men before I bought the app.

The U.S. Constitution is included in full — with the original Articles, all the Amendments, the signers (with bios), and scans of an original copy.

Something every Trivial Pursuit player and American high school student should have handy is the list of U.S. Presidents. They're listed in chronological order, and if you tap through on one of them (as I did with Thomas Jefferson) you get — as you can see in the figure to the right below — the dates they held office, birth and death dates (where applicable), spouse's name (where applicable), a list of other offices held, any nicknames (whether enjoyed or hated), and a list of this president's published works (where applicable).

Want more? There's a link to an in-app Store where you buy a searchable address book for government contracts, a collection of Enlightenment writings that were influential to the founding fathers, the writings of Thomas Jefferson and John Adams, and some documents about the U.S. flag. They're all $0.99 or $1.99, but I wish they were included with the basic app.

There's also a list of all 50 states (as of this writing) with information about current office holders and a link to each state's Web site; information about the current Supreme Court justices, as well as a collection of key Supreme Court rulings that have shaped this country.

Lastly, there's a list of another 16 documents that have been important to the shaping of the U.S.: The Articles of Confederation, Federalist Papers, the Emancipation Proclamation, the Civil Rights Act, the Louisiana Purchase Treaty, and more.

Best features

I'm a big believer in understanding as much as you can about your government, and the materials presented in this app will go a long way toward helping you understand key aspects of its founding and development.

Worst features

The information is crucial, but the interface itself wouldn't even crack the Top 50 of all the great apps we've featured in this book. Also, the additional content for sale should be included with the basic version, in my opinion.

The Elements — A Visual Exploration
$13.99

Nerd Alert! This app will help you get your geek on, whether you can recite the Periodic Table of Elements frontwards and backwards (bonus points if you know the 1959 song!), or whether you think Lawrencium is some Roman city you might have studied back in high school. No wait, I've got another: Or whether you think Dubnium is a new Electronica band from Sweden! Wait, one more: Or whether you think Bismuth is the capital of North Dakota! I could do this all day . . . because I'm a big dorky, geeky nerd.

But I won't. The Elements — A Visual Exploration is a wonderful app that offers a wonderful way to explore and learn more about the Periodic Table of the Elements. It features gorgeous photos and detailed information about each element, including background and historical details.

In fact, it's more than an app, it started out as a coffee-table book that the author turned into an interactive experience as an app.

This app has three main screens. The Home screen is the full Periodic Table. Each element is represented by either a 3D, rotating image of the element, or a picture of the person credited with discovering the element. Theoretical elements without final names have placeholder images while the scientific world hashes out what will be what.

At the bottom of the home screen is a button labeled Song. This is the awesome 1959 song by Tom Lehrer (with music by Gilbert and Sullivan!) where he sings the names of the elements. It's awesome, and you should listen to it!

Tap on one of those elements to be taken to a page with a large rotating image of the element in question. Sometimes those photos are of the element in its raw form, and some of them are photos of some sort of finished product. In addition to the photo, you'll find atomic information, boiling and melting points, crystalline structure, and more. You can tap a button in the bottom to go to a page with written information on the element.

Most of this data is supplied by WolframAlpha, the "Answer Engine" I write about a little later in this chapter.

If you tap one of the information panels, you'll get the WolframAlpha entry for the element, complete with more detailed numbers.

The figure below shows the information page for Gold. For this element, the author talks about its value (did you know that all the gold ever mined throughout human history would fit into a cube 60 feet on its edge? I didn't, until I got The Elements), why it's valued, commercial uses, and more. For the recently discovered elements, we learn about the discovery process, the discoverer, and more. Each element is a little different, and I spent a lot of time reading through these pages.

The best thing about the app, however, might just be the fact that you can rotate/spin all the objects in the figure below with a flick of your finger. I know, it sounds silly, but wait until you see it! You can also double-tap to get a bigger version of that image (which you can also spin! Yeah!).

Best features:

This app is cool-looking, has great information and amazing photography, and you can spin things!

Worst features:

Some will find the price tag of $13.99 to be on the expensive side, but it's worth it for an app so well designed, informative, and fun. Also, there's no portrait mode.

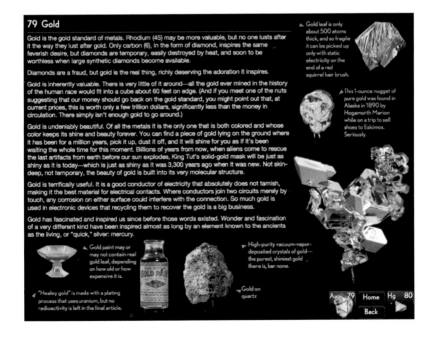

Wikipanion
Free

Wikipedia is great online resource, and you can access it all day long through Safari (or another browser) on your iPad. There are also several apps for browsing the site, and they offer some cool benefits — for example, Wikihood, which is specifically geared toward mining Wikipedia for information about what's near where you are (it's a great travel app!). Wikipanion is a more generalized app that allows you to browse all of Wikipedia; I picked it to feature in this chapter because I think it offers a better interface than the Web site itself, and a faster way to use the site.

Let's start at the top, literally. In the figure below, you'll see a search field in the top-right corner on the screen. If you tap that gear icon next to it, you get a pop-up window that allows you to do several things. The most important of those is to search the contents of the current page; it's like a "Find" search in a desktop browser. That's something you just can't currently do in Safari for iPad, and this feature alone makes this app a must-have if you're a frequent Wikipedia user. You can also use this tool to change your search to Wiktionary, e-mail a link to the current page, or open that page in Safari — and you can change the font and font size, too.

On the left side of the screen is a navigation panel. This panel includes a link to GeoNames for finding your current location and any Wikipedia entries near that location, as well as Wikipedia entries that are near the article you currently have open (where applicable). It also includes links relating the current article.

For instance, in the figure below we have an article about the Horezu Monastery in Romania. The app offers me links to an article about World Heritage sites in Romania, another article about Romanian Orthodox monasteries, and more.

It also offers me two links to lists of articles needing geo-coordinates. This sidebar will often include links like that for those who do their part to contribute or edit content in Wikipedia.

Lastly, this sidebar includes links to the home page of Wikipedia and a great Random Page button for . . . well . . . going on an adventure (to a random entry in Wikipedia)! If you're an information junkie like me, you might wonder where the time went if you start tapping that button. It's how I found the article on that monastery, in fact!

Other key features of the app include bookmarking favorite articles and downloading any images you come across to your photo library.

There's a paid version of the app called Wikipanion Plus for iPad ($4.99) that offers a queue for articles you want to read; you can also download articles for offline reading, and load articles in the background while you continue browsing.

Best features

Wikipanion offers faster browsing on Wikipedia, with an interface that is superior to the original Web site, simply by using a Web browser.

Worst features

I found a few bugs while working with the app — for example, the Twitter button only takes me to the Twitter app on my iPad without passing along links or other information about the current page. These bugs were rare, though, or this app wouldn't have made the cut for this chapter.

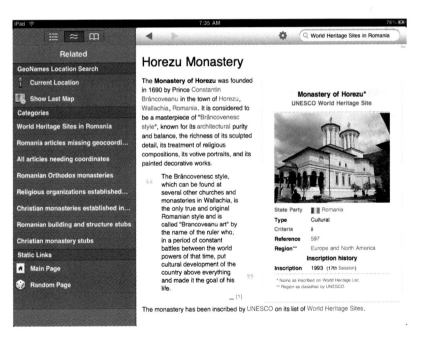

WolframAlpha
$0.99 — Hybrid

WolframAlpha is probably the most awesome thing on the Internet you aren't likely to have heard about yet. Often mistaken for a search engine, WolframAlpha is instead an . . . *answer* engine, for lack of a better term. With this service, you can find out lots of facts about lots of things, and you can also use it to solve advanced trigonometry and calculus problems. The company's iOS app is an interface for everything you can do through that Web site, but I think the app has a better interface — and for those doing higher math, the developers provided all those nifty Greek symbols right there on the onscreen keyboard.

If the name Wolfram rings a bell, you're either a fan of *Angel* or familiar with Mathematica, the flagship product of the parent company, Wolfram Research. Mathematica is the big dog in the world of scientific calculation software, and it also happens to provide the computational power behind the WolframAlpha Web site and iPad app.

Let's start with what kind of information you can get from WolframAlpha. There's the math stuff I already mentioned, but that's just a tiny part of more than 10 trillion pieces of data the company claims to have stored in its servers. What kind of data is that? Well, it's things like atomic weights, population figures, dates, calorie content, latitude and longitude coordinates, heights, depths, market caps and other stock information, employee counts, population figures, crossword clues for individual words, Scrabble-score values (no, seriously), etymology information, weather info, tax rates, and on and on and on. And the app allows you to mine that enormous database to get answers.

This is another one of those apps that I think works a lot better in landscape mode, but I took screenshots in portrait mode so I could show you two of them.

For instance, if I enter "Cupertino," I get the information you can see in the figure to the left below: Economic properties, current weather, elevation, its county, and even a list of famous people born there (not seen is a map of the U.S. and a local map). If I entered "closest city Cupertino," I would have gotten just that list of three nearby cities. "Elevation Cupertino" would have returned only that. Entering "Gold" returns atomic weight info, its melting and boiling points, density, electrical type, atomic radius, its half-life (Trick question! It's stable!), and a lot more. "Distance between San Francisco and NYC," tells me it's 2,578 miles, with travel times for jet and sound (again, seriously), and even what fraction of the Earth's circumference that distance is (1/10th).

And, of course, there's the math stuff. Check out the figure to the right below for an example of using WolframAlpha to solve a calculus equation. You can enter any kind of equation and WolframAlpha will do the calculations for you.

That huge massive keyboard that takes up most of the screen includes all manner of symbols used in calculus. The middle section is always shown when you tap the input field, but the upper section can be shown or hidden as needed.

Best features

WolframAlpha is an amazingly powerful "answer engine" you can use to get a wide variety of information.

Worst features

You have to figure out how to enter your queries to get the information you're looking for, but that's not too big a hurdle. You can't tap on anything in the results for more information.

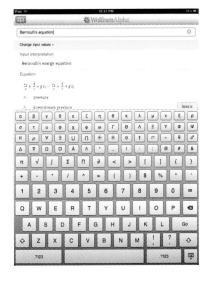

World Atlas HD
$1.99

Did you have a giant atlas in your house when you were a kid? Or maybe you used the atlases in your school library to learn more about foreign lands? Or maybe you're not a geezer like me and you just expect the world to be at your fingertips thanks to the magic of the Internet. Whatever the case, if you have any interest in knowing about the countries that lie beyond the borders of your own, you're going to like World Atlas HD. For $1.99, it puts beautiful maps and information about hundreds of countries a tap away — plus you can put virtual pins on your maps to mark the countries you've read up on — or (if you're a real globetrotter) the places you've visited!

Launch this app and you're presented with a map of planet. You're offered a "Tutorial" that simply explains that you can tap, double-tap, pinch, and zoom, and that you can change maps by using the Map Library button. It's not much of a tutorial, but the app is simple enough to use to begin with.

Maps are accessed through the Internet, but once they're downloaded, they're stored on your iPad. With that in mind, I took the time to download all the maps right from the beginning. You have to do them one at a time, but you'll get faster access the first time you want to actually use them — and you'll be able to access all the maps offline.

Well, not *all* the maps will be available offline, just the Executive and Political maps for the globe and the individual continents, as well as the first layer of the global Satellite map. The Road and detailed Satellite maps are provided by Bing, and require a connection to the Internet to use.

Check out the figure to the right below. I'm in the Executive style map of the globe, and I've used the pins to mark some of the places I've been to. At the bottom of the screen are three buttons that allow me to switch among the three different map styles, Executive, Political, and Satellite. The Executive and Political maps show the same thing, but I like the muted colors of the Executive style better; they're easier to read. The Satellite view offers just that, a satellite view without borders or country names. Switching between the styles is seamless once you've downloaded all the maps.

In the figure to the right below, I've used the Nations menu to find Australia quickly. The information panel gives me a brief history of the county/continent (it's both in this case), information about the fauna, the biggest cities, several stats (which you can see in the figure), and then a breakdown of Industries, Agriculture, and Exports. I could zoom in all the way to a street-level view, though that requires the Internet connection to get Bing maps.

Best features

It's a world atlas for less than two bucks on a device that makes finding and reading about different countries far easier than with a printed book (though I *like* books, so don't write to me thinking that I'm coming down on books!).

Worst features

I'm not a big fan of Bing's mapping services, and would prefer Google's. Your mileage may vary. Also, I think the app needs more information on all the countries it includes, though what's there will satisfy many people.

Google Mobile App
Free — Hybrid

Voice search on Google's search engine? Heck, if that's all Google Mobile App offered, that's all I'd need to recommend it. Tap the microphone and speak whatever it is you want to search for. The app records what you say, sends it to Google's sever farm for processing, and spits out the results faster than you can say antidisestablishmentarianism (in other words, pretty fast, but not instantaneous). It works very well, as long as you don't have a lot of ambient noise or a fan blowing past the iPad's microphone. This hybrid app also offers one-tap access to the host of online services known as Google Apps, but it does so by taking you to Safari.

Math Ref
$0.99 — Hybrid

Imagine being able to put crib notes for all the mathematical formulas you need on the inside of your palm. Now imagine if your palm was the size a huge serving platter, and you could put all the formulas on it that you're ever going to need — now or any time in the future. That's basically what Math Ref is: a repository of more than 1,400 "formulas, figures, tips and examples" for math, physics, chemistry, and more. Broken down into 18 categories, the app allows you to bookmark favorites and search for any terms you want defined. Now, if you can only get your teacher to let you use your iPad during that test!

Merriam-Webster's Collegiate Dictionary, Eleventh Edition
$24.99 — Hybrid

That price tag puts this app on the expensive side — especially if you're talking apps for college students — but the power of having some 250,000 definitions (words and phrases) on a device like the iPad makes it a solid investment for any student. This app offers an advantage over a print dictionary, too: You can do wildcard searches. You can use question marks (?) to substitute for specific letters or an asterisk (*) to substitute for an unknown number of letters. You can also search for similar words (though there's no thesaurus), and you can make in-app purchases to get additional dictionaries in English, French, and Spanish.

Moon Atlas
$5.99

Moon Atlas is a great app with which to study the Moon. The app offers a view of the visible side of the Moon, with major features labeled (double-tap a label for information about that feature). The farther you zoom in, the more labels appear, allowing you to get information about craters that are quite small (on a planetary scale). You'll even find the locations of man-made lunar landers and other equipment! Plus, you can use the app to see the moon as it looks from anywhere on Earth. Lastly, you get Moon phase information that you can swipe through to go backward and forward in time. It's cool!

Starwalk for iPad — Interactive Astronomy Guide
$4.99

I've gushed about this app frequently and often, and this seems like a good place to do so again. Starwalk for iPad puts the stars at your fingertips, literally. If you hold up your iPad, it will show you precisely what stars, constellations, and planets are in that part of the sky — whether or not you can see them with your naked eye. You can get detailed information on those stars, and you can drill farther away in the sky just by tapping, allowing you to get the goods on thousands of stars. Then there's the Picture of the Day, awesome photos and images of distant places in the galaxy, the night sky, and more.

13 Social Networking

AIM for iPad
Free

Who'da thunk that AOL would release a really good iPad app? "AOL" doesn't exactly leap into my mind when I think of companies well versed in excellent user interface design, but AIM for iPad is pretty darned good!

 AIM stands for AOL Instant Messenger. It was originally an internal part of AOL's online subscription service. At some point the company released it as an open standard so people outside of AOL could chat with each other and with AOL users; the idea was to compete with Yahoo! Instant Messenger and other chat systems. Today, AOL is the network behind Apple's iChat service, and you can find any number of third-party AIM clients for Windows and Mac.

Let's look at the figure below. This is the main interface for AIM for iPad. On the left are all my active IMs; on the right is my Buddy List, with the category breakdowns I originally set up in iChat stored as preferences on AIM's servers. In the middle is a conversation I had with *The Mac Observer*'s Managing Editor, Jeff Gamet. We're discussing the fact that the smiley emoticon in this app doesn't look so hot.

 AIM for iPad includes support for Facebook Connect and Twitter — which means you can use the app to chat with your friends who are logged on to Facebook and get Twitter posts, too.

If I tap the button in the upper-left corner of the screen, I can log out and switch to AIM, Facebook, MobileMe, or .Mac, but no matter what kind of account you're using, the app allows you to chat with anyone logged on to Facebook, AIM, AOL, ICQ, or Apple's .Mac/MobileMe network.

If I tap the chat-bubble icon in the upper-right corner of the screen, I get more options. I can view my Lifestream, which is all the status updates anyone on my Buddy List has made; it will also grab Facebook status updates and Twitter updates. You can filter those status updates according to 13 different criteria — see (for example) just those updates with photos, or just those updates from Facebook, or however you slice it. You can also manage your AIM status updates and notifications from this screen.

AIM for iPad comes with two dozen wallpaper themes. In the figure below I've chosen the "Tunnel" theme, though I think I prefer using the app with a solid background color.

Lastly, you can send an IM out as an SMS text message to a cell phone via Wi-Fi or 3G.

Best features

It's AIM on your iPad! The interface makes good use of the screen real estate, and there are many options. I think a lot of people will also appreciate the ability to chat with Facebook friends and AIM buddies in one app.

Worst features

You can't add your own themes, and I'd like the ability to simply have solid backgrounds in the individual panes (there are Solid Colors themes that partially accomplish that). Twitter support is incomplete (notably no retweeting and no Direct Messages).

Emoti HD for Facebook
$2.99 — Hybrid

The iPad is a great social-networking device. For instance, you're sure to meet people if you use yours in public! But seriously, in the same way that it's a great device for Web browsing, e-mail, and reading e-books, your iPad makes for a great way to browse and post to Facebook, Twitter, and other forms of social networking. With Emoti HD, you can use your iPad to add great-looking emoticons when you post to Facebook — which not only imparts more information about your post (in the way of visual clues), it can even help your posts stand out from everyone else's.

An Emoticon is one of those little sideways faces you can make out of text characters, like :) for a "smiley face" or : (for a "sad face." Emoji, on the other hand, started in Japan as a system for including actual images for smiley (and other) faces through SMS text messages. Emoti HD's name is a juxtaposition of the two concepts.

Emoti HD for Facebook currently has 186 emoticons that were custom-made by the developer. They look great on both your iPad's display and on Facebook in any browser. The app has all the basic emoticons for being happy, angry, sad, ecstatic, crying, proud, goofy, surprised, in love, and even sleepy. There are also emoticons for sports, saying "thank you," weather, military, food, music, gambling, religion, and many more, as you can see in the figure to the left below.

You can also use Emoti HD to post without using an emoticon. On the first page, you'll find a dotted box with the text "no emoti" in it. Tap that, share your post, and it will have no smiley (just like a normal Facebook post).

To make a post, tap an emoticon to get a keyboard and entry field, as you can see in the figure to the right below. You can pick your destination (your Wall, a friend's Wall, Group, Page, or Fan Page) by tapping the second field labeled Wall. Write the post, tap Share, and you're done! It's very easy to use.

On your first post, you'll have a Facebook Connect button you tap to log in to Facebook from the app. If you need to change accounts, you can log out of the current account by tapping the From field in a new post.

Emoti HD for Facebook also allows you to arrange the pages of icons as you see fit. Tap the icon with the little squares in the upper-right corner of the screen, and you'll get something like the figure to the left below. Tap and hold one of those pages and they'll all begin to shake, just as your app icons shake when you're rearranging them on your iPad's home screen. You can then tap and drag a page of icons to wherever you want them. For instance, I'm not a big soccer/football fan, so I moved those emoticons to the end.

Best features

Great-looking emoticons really jazz up your Facebook posts!

Worst features

Great-looking emoticons really jazz up your Facebook posts! No, seriously: Some people hate that sort of thing.

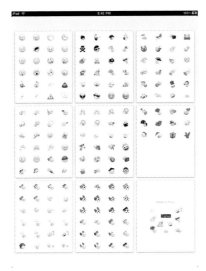

Friendly — Facebook Browser
$0.99

If you're looking for more of a Facebook-like way to use the service on your iPad, you can use the company's iPhone app or you can use Friendly — Facebook Browser. The advantage of Friendly is that it offers an interface built for the iPad. There are a few iPad apps on the App Store built for browsing Facebook, but until Facebook itself releases one, Friendly is going to offer you the best experience (Social is another good choice).

The main page for the app is where you get your news feed from all your Facebook Friends. In the figure to the left below, you'll see posts from some of my friends — as well as three tabs: News Feed, Events, and Places.

 You can toggle the News Feed tab to display your Live Feed. You access it by tapping the toggle in that tab, which changes the label to red text that reads *Live Feed*.

For posts in your News Feed or Live Feed, you can add comments or tap the Like button just as you would in a browser. Tap an image that one of your Friends posted, and you'll pull it up full-screen. Tap that full-screen image, and you get some navigation buttons on either side that allow you to browse through your Friend's other images.

The Events tab displays any upcoming Events for Pages or Groups that you've joined, and the Places tab uses Location Services on your iPad to show you Facebook Friends in the nearby area.

At the very top of the screen are buttons to take you to your Profile — where you can see your own Wall, view (but not edit) your personal info, and see the Photos you've uploaded to Facebook. There you can also see a list of your Friends, view your Pages, and manage your Inbox. The icon just to the right of your Inbox takes you to a screen with all recent Notifications (such as any comments made on your posts), and pending Requests you might have.

 There's an in-app browser for pulling up articles that your Friends link to — and you won't have to leave the app to read the content those external links make available.

In the figure to the left below, you'll see two chat bubbles in the lower-right corner of the screen. If I tap that, I can see which of my friends is online and chat with them. In the figure to the right below, you'll see a conversation I had with Shawn King from the *Your Mac Life* podcast about Macworld Conference & Expo. My Facebook friends who are online are listed in the pane on the left side of the screen; our chat is on the right. It's hardly the best chat client on the app store — but it gets the job done!

In short, it's Facebook — but you may have noticed two things I haven't mentioned: Facebook games and ads. Neither one is offered in the app — Friendly is focused on interacting with your Friends.

Best features

Friendly offers most of the Facebook experience (no games, but also no ads), and it does so on a way built for the iPad — not for a browser, and not for the iPhone.

Worst features

I've encountered a few bugs now and then when using the app, but not enough to push me into browsing Facebook in a browser.

Twitter
Free — Hybrid

I love the Twitter iOS app. It's one of those apps that I think sets the bar on usability, like E*TRADE Mobile, NPR for iPad, Pages, StockWatch, and some of the others I've singled out for their awesomeness in the GUI department. I suppose I shouldn't be surprised. The app was developed by Loren Brichter, who originally developed Tweetie for iPhone and Mac OS X. Both apps were so highly regarded that Twitter, the company, bought Tweetie for iPhone and hired Mr. Brichter to turn it into a new app called simply Twitter (Tweetie for Mac OS X is still available as of this writing).

Now, Twitter is a hybrid app for iPhone and iPad, and I think it offers the single best Twitter experience on either device. From usability to readability, general layout, and design, it's a great app; most other apps could only hope to be as well designed as this one.

Let's look at the figure to the left below. In portrait mode, you get two panels (I like landscape mode better, but wanted to show you two screenshots). The left panel has a list of your Twitter accounts with tabs for your Timeline (tweets from you and those you follow), @Mentions (tweets with your @Name in them), Lists, Direct Messages, and a tab for viewing and editing your own Profile, and one for Searching. To the right is a pane for your tweets. At the bottom of the page is a Settings button and a New Tweet button.

All those elements are logically laid out, but what sets this app apart is the way those elements can be expanded, pushed, pinched, and swiped — making the best use of your screen real estate at any given time. For instance, if I tap one of the tweets in my Timeline, a third panel comes out from the right, squeezing everything over to the left. In the figure to the right below, you'll see how it expands to an information pane about the person who posted the tweet — with bio, location, URL (if the user filled out that info), and links to all of his or her tweets, @Mentions, and favorites. You can also Follow or Unfollow that person with one tap.

If the tweet you tapped is part of a conversation or a hashtag chain, Twitter pulls all the posts from that chain and displays them in chronological order. It's easy to follow conversations that might have taken place over hours, or even days!

TIP

Another way to get someone's information pane is to use two fingers to expand a tweet. You'll get a pop-up window with the tweet, reply options, and the personal info I mentioned already.

You can reply, repost, quote, translate (seriously, one-tap translation!), or just copy a link that shows up in a tweet to your iPad clipboard.

Lastly, there's a built-in browser for displaying photos and links. At the bottom of the browser is a button that lets you open the link in Safari.

Best features

Great interface, excellent user experience and use of screen real estate. Twitter on the iPad is the best way I've found to use Twitter yet.

Worst features

Links show up as gray text in your Timeline, the same color as hashmarks. They get highlighted in a blue square when you tap a tweet, but I think they should be displayed in blue text in the Timeline.

Twittelator for iPad — Twitter Client
$4.99

Twittelator for iPad was developed by Stone Design, a company that has been making Mac OS X apps since before it was Mac OS X. The company started out developing for NeXTStep — and that means doing things the Apple way is deeply embedded in the company's DNA.

For those who don't remember (or didn't know), NeXT was the company Steve Jobs formed when he was ousted from Apple, and it was (perhaps ironically) the company that Apple ended up buying in 1997 in order to make NeXTStep the successor to the original Mac OS. With NeXTStep as the foundation, Mac OS X was born, and Mac OS X is, in turn, the foundation of iOS.

And that's probably why this app has such a nice fit and finish, and why it's so easy to use. Let's look at the main interface. In portrait mode, you get one pane of information and a navigation bar for viewing tweets from your friends, Direct Messages, @Mentions, Channels, Search, Lists, Drafts, and More (Profile, Retweets, Trends, Everyone, and Settings).

Under the More tab you'll find a button for seeing Trends, which is short for Trending Topics. These are topics that have recently increased in frequency/popularity within the Twitter community, and a lot of people find it interesting to see what's becoming popular. For instance, on the night that I wrote this, Lady Gaga's dress made out of meat for her VMA appearance was all the rage. She, Justin Bieber, and Jared Leto. Gotta love pop culture!

In the figure to the left below, you'll see I'm looking at tweets from my Facebook Friends. I'm showing a tweet from Michael Gartenberg to show one of the features I love about this app: The images people tweet are shown inline. I love that! If I want to see a larger image, I can tap the current image or its link to open the in-app browser. In the figure to the right below, you'll see one of the Lists I follow (`mac-iphone-dev`). The way Twittelator separates these functions makes for a very clean interface. On the other hand, there's a lot of unused screen real estate that I think could be put to better use.

In landscape mode you get two panes — one with your Timeline of tweets, along with the larger one you get in portrait mode. This addresses some, but not all, of my complaints about unused space.

Other features allow you to follow other users' Lists, create and manage a queue of Draft tweets, and browse a list of Channels that contain posts about specific topics (Business, Arts, Health, Food, Politics, and more).

I made it pretty clear in my writeup about Twitter (see above) that I prefer that app, but this is the kind of thing where different people like different things, and Twittelator is another great choice on your iPad.

Best features

This app has a super-clean interface that works well in both landscape and portrait mode. I also love that photos are displayed in-line with their posts. The browser integration is also excellent.

Worst features

Twittelator for iPad looks great, but there's a lot of unused screen real estate, especially in portrait mode. I'm all for a clean interface, but I'd like to be able to at least expand the individual windows if I want to.

BeejiveIM for iPad
$9.99

BeejiveIM for iPad is toward the expensive side of social-networking apps at $9.99, but the company is positioning the app as a premium product with reliable connections to all the major IM networks, low CPU overhead, and a good interface. It supports AIM and Apple's iChat, MSN, Yahoo!, GoogleTalk, Facebook IM, ICQ, Jabber, and MySpace IM. It also features real-time chats, group chats, file transfers, SMS out, emoticons, push notifications, and more. It is, in short, a one-stop shop for all your Instant Messaging needs! I should also note that the app's fans swear by it and say it is well worth the money!

Tumbleroo
$4.99

Tumbleroo is an app for working with Tumblr, the blogging service that bridges the social-networking world. As with several other browser-based online services, Tumbleroo's app-based interface offers a better way to use the host service than does a Web page. The app includes full support for the Tumblr dashboard (including support for audio and video posts); you can also indicate that you like posts from other users and "reblog" content that bears repeating. Tumbleroo also allows users to manage multiple accounts, create private posts, and to send their posts to Twitter (or not).

Qubical
$0.99 — Hybrid

I picked this app as much for its unique approach to accessing Facebook content as anything else. With Qubical, you see all your Facebook friends not as names in a list or in a time line, but as faces on a 3D cube that you can zoom in on and rotate. Tap one of the images on the cube to pull up the name of a particular Friend, double-tap it to pull up that Friend's status updates or to write on his or her wall! It's a very different way of browsing Facebook, and I think it will appeal to people who are more spatially or visually oriented.

textPlus Free Text + Unlimited FREE App-To-App Messaging Worldwide

Free — Hybrid

This app with the absurdly long name is for a service centered on bringing the world of chat rooms to mobile instant messaging. If you've ever spent time in an AOL chat room, you'll know what I'm talking about. If not, here's the gist: Chat rooms are virtual places where multiple people type in lines of text to talk with one another. With this app, you can find existing chat rooms, create your own, or simply send SMS text messages from your iPad to an SMS-enabled mobile phone, or to other textPlus users. The interface is nice (it has some Apple iChat-like elements), and it's easy to use. If you miss chat rooms, check it out.

TweetDeck for iPad

Free

I have one more Twitter app to tell you about: TweetDeck. This app is well suited for people who follow more people on Twitter than they actually have time to follow — or even for people who simply need to prioritize their followers. With TweetDeck's multi-column view, you can make new columns that correspond to specific people. For instance, if you have some work-related accounts that you need to make sure you see, make a column for them. Although lists of tweets have achieved a similar result since TweetDeck was first released, you can have as many columns/categories of tweets as you need — and simply swipe through them as needed.

14 Travel, Navigation, and Weather

Bill Atkinson PhotoCard
$4.99

 To some, Bill Atkinson is the legendary Apple software engineer who created MacPaint and HyperCard. To others, he's a world-renowned nature photographer. Bill Atkinson PhotoCard is an iPad (and iPhone) app that shows off his brilliance in both disciplines.

The PhotoCard app lets you create absolutely gorgeous high-resolution postcards and send them from your iPad via your choice of either e-mail or the U.S. Postal Service.

It couldn't be easier to create a postcard. You start by choosing an image. You can use one of the 150 Bill Atkinson nature photos included with the app, some of which are shown on the left side of the image on the left below. Or you can select any of your own pictures from the iPad's Photos app.

 With Apple's iPad Camera Connection Kit ($29; see Chapter 19) you can import your own photos and videos from most digital cameras via USB cable or from an SD card. This feature makes it really easy to create and send professional-looking postcards with pictures of family members, landmarks, or whatever you like.

When you've selected a picture, you can customize your postcard, using over 150 different stamps (such as the tree of lights on the right side of the image on the left below) and more than 300 different stickers, some of which are shown in the image on the right below. And you have a choice of dozens of fonts for the text on your postcard.

If you're going to send your message via e-mail, you can even add a voice recording of up to 60 seconds to your postcard.

The thing I like best about Bill Atkinson PhotoCard is that the cards sent via U.S. Postal Service are gorgeous. They're 8.25 by 5.5 inches, printed with a state-of-the-art HP Indigo digital press on high-quality glossy photo paper.

Sending your postcard via e-mail is always free — but sending printed cards via U.S. Mail is not. You get one free printed postcard with the $4.99 app, with additional print-and-mail credits available as an in-app purchase. The more credits you buy, the lower the cost per card you mail. At press time, those costs were $1.50 to $2.00 for cards mailed to addresses in the USA and $2.25 to $3.00 for cards mailed to international addresses.

If you just want to see how the app works, there's a free version called *Bill Atkinson PhotoCard Lite*. It has the exact same features as the $4.99 version but comes with just 10 nature pictures, 10 stamps, and 20 stickers. And, of course, it doesn't include a free printed postcard. So if you only want to use your own photos and send your postcards via e-mail, the Lite version will serve your needs.

Best features

It couldn't be easier to use, and it includes awesome nature photos, stamps, and stickers. And having the option to send a voice recording via e-mail is terrific.

Worst features

Although the mailed postcards are gorgeous, they can take a week or more to arrive at their destination.

FlightTrack Pro
$9.99 US

This app brings out the geek in me, and I bet it will do the same thing for you. As the name suggests, its main purpose is to track flights, in real time, with updated statuses, or even on a map. How cool is that? In addition, it pushes alerts out to you for changes in flight information — and remembers the flights you've entered so you don't have to enter them again. The app also offers integration with TripIt to fetch your personal flight itineraries automagically without your having to enter a thing.

Let's start with the basic features: I've chosen three random flights to monitor, and the app keeps them in a list for me until I delete them, as shown in the figure on the left below. For quick updates, all the basic information I need is right there. For instance, for the three flights I'm currently monitoring, I see that all three are en route. I have flight numbers, departure and arrival times, and the departure and destination cities.

If I tap one of the flights — in this case, the Toronto to San Francisco flight shown in the figure on the right below— I see an overlay with the terminals, gate numbers, arrival and departure times, and even the baggage claim carousel. As you see, this flight will reach the gate in San Francisco 42 minutes late. If I had enabled FlightTrack Pro's Sounds and Alerts (in Settings⇨Notifications⇨Flight Track Pro), I'd have seen an onscreen alert and heard a distinctive alert sound to tell me the flight was running late. For me, this may be the best thing about the app — important information about flights I'm tracking is displayed onscreen, even if I'm using a different app. When I have to pick someone up at the airport, this is a heck of a lot better (and easier) than calling the airline or even looking it up on the Web.

The status area in the upper-right corner of this overlay — it says 28,700 feet in the figure on the right below — rotates through flight status, elevation (shown), and speed.

In both of the figures below, you can see a map which shows you not only where, exactly, the airplane currently is, but also weather radar (the green and yellow splotches in the South and Midwest) so you know if your loved ones are flying through serious weather conditions. How cool is that?

And you can choose which flights are displayed on the map by tapping the little eyeball to the right of each flight in the FlightTrack overlay. This is particularly helpful if you're tracking multiple flights and want to focus on a certain one.

Other features include the capability to e-mail flight info directly from the app. The e-mails have the latest flight status (including updated arrival times) and a still from the same map I have below! Alternatively, I could tweet the current flight status through the built-in Twitter support.

This is a very slick app with sophisticated flight-tracking capabilities. If you fly a lot, or if your colleagues or loved ones fly a lot, you'll want this app. If $9.99 is more than you want to pay, for $4.99, you can get the regular version of FlightTrack without the push alerts, airport delay notifications, or support for TripIt.

In the course of testing this app, I created a free account on TripIt.com so I could try this feature. The feature is automatically retrieving all of your flight information for all of your trips from TripIt.com. Which rocks. If you travel often, TripIt could be a terrific time and effort saver, even if you don't choose to buy this app. I love being able to forward confirmation e-mail to TripIt, which adds the flight(s) automatically. It's free, so check it out at www.tripit.com.

Best features

The push alerts for any kind of flight status change are really helpful, especially with so many late flights these days.

Worst features

It's occasionally less accurate than airline Web sites.

Inrix Traffic/Inrix Traffic Pro

Free/$9.99 per year or $24.99 for life

Inrix Traffic is a free app that provides real-time traffic information and traffic forecasts. It's easy to use, and I use it all the time to avoid traffic any time I drive more than a few miles from home.

The real-time traffic-flow information it delivers covers major road-ways in 126 cities across the U.S. and Canada and, at least according to its publisher, Inrix is the source for traffic information used by Ford, BMW, and the U.S. Department of Transportation (to name a few large organizations).

The flow of traffic appears on a familiar Google Map you can pinch or unpinch to zoom into or out of. Traffic moving at or near the speed limit is displayed in green, as are most of the major highways shown in the figure on the left below. Moderate traffic is displayed in orange; heavy traffic is shown in red. Traffic incidents — such as construction, road closures, concerts, conventions, sporting events, and so on — are depicted by icons such as the yellow traffic cone just above the river next to the traffic slowdown on Highway 290/35. When you tap these icons, you'll see an overlay with details of the incident.

Much of the information in the incident detail overlays is crowd-sourced, so it includes the time and date the incident was reported, as well as confirmation from other drivers if available. I've found the incident reports to be mostly reliable, though they sometimes appear for a while after the incident has been cleared.

Another useful feature is traffic prediction. The app analyzes current traffic conditions, time of day, day of the week, holidays, accidents, construction, conventions, sporting events, and more, using the data to predict traffic situations over the next few hours.

Everything I've mentioned so far is available for free and with no advertising. That's good, but while the app delivers a lot of value for free, you'll probably want to upgrade to the Pro version for $9.99 a year or $24.99 for life. I am very satisfied with my Pro purchase, which adds access to even better and more useful features such as:

- **Fastest route:** Calculates the fastest route from Point A to Point B, on the basis of the same criteria used to predict traffic flow in the free version.

- **Expected travel time and ETA:** Calculates how long it will take you to drive from Point A to Point B and your estimated time of arrival (ETA).

✔ **Directions:** Provides turn-by-turn directions onscreen, available as arrows on the map as well as a textual list of turns.

✔ **Best time to leave:** Calculates the best time to leave Point A so you arrive at Point B with the shortest drive time.

✔ **Save frequent destinations and favorite routes:** This feature is worth the price of admission to me. It lets me save all my frequent destinations in a list (as shown in the image on the right below) so I can obtain the fastest route, expected travel time, ETA, best time to leave, and directions (which I don't need since I go to these places regularly).

✔ **Traffic cameras:** There aren't that many of them and the pictures are often pixilated and grainy, but they're available and can be useful sometimes.

I'd be remiss if I didn't mention Beat the Traffic HD, another free app that displays live traffic maps and incidents. It doesn't offer the Pro features that make Inrix Traffic a winner for me, but if you're just looking for a decent free traffic app, you might prefer Beat the Traffic HD.

Best features

Most of the Pro features, especially saving frequent destinations.

Worst features

Information provided is not always 100% reliable.

MotionX GPS Drive HD
$2.99

MotionX GPS Drive HD is the iPad version of one of my two favorite voice-guided GPS apps on the iPhone. My other fave on the iPhone, Navigon MobileNavigator, isn't even available for the iPad — and at $59.99 (for the iPhone app), it's hard to recommend it over MotionX GPS Drive HD anyway.

I'm surprised that Navigon and other voice-guided GPS apps for the iPhone aren't available for the iPad yet; the iPad's huge screen makes it a much better vehicle (ha ha) for navigation apps than the iPhone.

Before I start raving about how much I like this app, let me say that when you buy this app for $2.99, you receive a 30-day Live Voice Guidance package at no additional cost. But when that expires, you'll pay an additional $2.99 for 30 days or $24.99 for a one-year Live Voice Guidance package. While that may sound like a bad deal, it's actually quite good for you. I find I only need Voice Guidance every two or three months, so my total cost for using this app for a year might be as low as $14.95 (5 × $2.99). Some of the voice-guided navigation apps for the iPhone cost $60, $70, $80, or more.

Okay. On top of being a great value, MotionX GPS Drive HD offers seven things I find particularly compelling:

- ✔ The maps and onscreen instructions are extremely clear and easy to understand, as you can see in the figure on the left below. Notice that all the street names are extremely easy to read — and the instructions (the next turn is a left in 0.1 mi onto Rosewood Ave) are crystal clear.

- ✔ The MotionX-3D Plus maps always show the name of the street you're currently on at the bottom of the screen (Chicon St. in the image on the left below).

- ✔ If I don't need Live Voice Guidance for a month, I don't have to pay for it. I buy it when I need it, with no recurring fees or subscription.

- ✔ The app itself is under 10MB, and it lets you decide how much storage space you want to use for maps; other navigation apps weigh in at 1.5GB or more!

- ✔ It features "Smart Router" technology that uses multiple traffic-data sources to calculate the best route in real time.

- ✔ It's the only GPS navigation package I've tested that offers two simulation modes — step-by-step or automatic at playback speeds up to 8X. I love this feature because it lets me see the entire route, turn by turn, so I'm familiar with where I'm going before I even get into my car. And best of all, these simulations don't require an active Live Voice Guidance package.

✔ It's easy to use, with all its features available from a single screen, as shown in the figure on the right below.

The Search interface is nicely designed, offering categories like coffee shops, gas and service stations, dining, and a browse mode that shows you nearby entertainment, restaurant, shopping, and WiFi hotspot options. Plus, you can search during an active navigation session and see results that are on your chosen route.

I wish I had room for another image because I would love to show you the way MotionX GPS Drive HD shows you what lane(s) you should be in as you approach multi-lane freeway interchanges. The arrows are big and easy to understand at a glance, so you can get into the proper lane with time to spare.

Best features

Just about every MotionX GPS Drive HD feature is first-class — and the app is updated frequently; the current version is the fifth major update since the app's initial release.

Worst features

You can only install it on 3G iPads, so if you have a Wi-Fi-only iPad, you're out of luck, even if you have a MyFi or other mobile Wi-Fi hotspot technology.

WeatherBug/WeatherBug Elite
Free

I bet I check the outside temperature on my iPad more than I do anything else. If I want to know how to dress, I've found that the iPad is hands down the fastest way to get outside weather conditions. But the iPad doesn't include a weather app. WeatherBug Elite is a wonderful substitute, providing useful weather info such as the temperature, conditions, forecast (seven-day and hourly!), alerts from the National Weather Service, access to live weathercams, cached information for viewing offline, satellite and radar maps . . . the list goes on. I tell you, this is a great weather app.

Check out the figure on the left below. It's my hometown of Austin, Texas, where it's 85 degrees as I'm writing this. In addition to temperature, I see the current conditions, wind direction and speed, heat index, dew point, and humidity. And in the middle of the screen is a more verbose forecast for today and the rest of the week (I'd flick upward to see the forecasts for Sunday through next Tuesday).

To see this seven-day forecast, I tapped the small Forecast panel near the top-right corner of the screen, which expanded it to front and center as shown. If you swipe left on the panels near the top of the screen (Conditions, Camera, and Forecast), the Hourly Forecast, Alerts, and Video panels appear.

You can watch multiple cities, too. Tap the blue circle with a white triangle next to the city name at the top of the screen to add whatever cities you want. The app automatically defaults to your current location if you allow the app to use Location Services on your iPad. WeatherBug Elite offers both U.S. and international locations, although not all of its services are available outside the U.S.

Near the bottom of the screen is the Maps Settings menu, which lets you choose to display Doppler Radar (shown in the figure on the right below), satellite imagery, and other variables such as temperature, humidity, and pressure levels, as overlays on the map.

My favorite feature of all is that you can animate most of the Map Settings options, which loops the last two hours of data so you can easily see if a storm is headed your way.

Other features of WeatherBug Elite include a daily weather video from the WeatherBug Web site (www.weatherbug.com) that offers a forecast and weather recap from a weather person. You can find that in the Video panel. Unfortunately, it's a national look at U.S. weather, so it's no substitute for your local TV station's weather segment, but you can pull it up on demand, which is handy.

If you swipe on the three visible weather widgets at the top of the screen — Conditions, Camera, and Forecast in the figure on the left, and Hourly Forecast, Alerts, and Video in the figure on the right — you'll see three more weather widgets. That alone is worth the price of admission but it gets even better. If you press and drag any of the six weather widgets to the left or right, you can change the order in which they appear and which three appear when you launch the app.

Finally, take note of the Camera panel, top center on the images below. With it you can look at the view from weather cameras installed in your watched cities. Just swipe your finger across the current image to move to another live camera view.

There are two other free weather apps I really like — Accu Weather for iPad and The Weather Channel Max. All three offer pretty much the same info, and while it was a very close race, I prefer WeatherBug Elite's elegant simplicity.

Best features

This app offers comprehensive weather coverage at your fingertips. It's like having a meteorologist in your pocket!

Worst features

Some international cities listed in the app don't have weather stations.

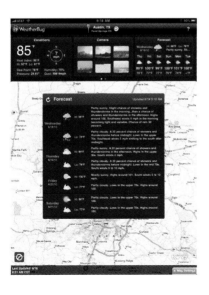
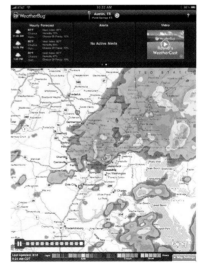

Google Earth
Free

The Google Earth app for iPad offers users the same astonishing satellite views of (most of) the planet as the company's desktop Google Earth map, and I think that's just amazing. Covering "half the world's population" and "a third of the earth's land mass," Google Earth for iPad lets you spin a globe to pick a spot, and then drill all the way down to a street-level view of that location. It's too cool, and you need to try it to believe it. The globe spins, you can turn on access to geo-located Wikipedia articles, and even see geo-located photographs from around the world if you turn on the Panoramio feature.

KAYAK Explore + Flight Search
Free

When I travel, the first Web site I visit is Kayak.com., where I can search hundreds of travel sites at once, making it quick and easy to compare prices. And the KAYAK Explore + Flight Search is faster and easier than visiting the site with Safari on your iPad, and it makes sorting, filtering, and comparing travel prices easy and fun. Be sure you check out the Explore button, which lets you specify a date range, activities you like (such as golf, skiing, gambling, and such), climate, maximum flight time, and price range — and then the app displays your options on a map!

WiFiGet HD
$2.99

No matter where you are, if you need to find a Wi-Fi hotspot, you need WiFiGet HD. This clever app has over 150,000 free Wi-Fi hotspots pre-installed, so you can search for a hotspot without an Internet connection. That's huge! And when you do have a wireless connection, it can access a database with over 200,000 free and paid hotspots. Of course, you can search for hotspots near your current location, but you can also search for them by address or by scrolling the map and looking for green pins (free hotspots) or red pins (paid hotspots). With hotels charging an arm and a leg for Internet access, WiFiGet HD will pay for itself the first time you use it.

Wikihood/Wikihood Plus
Free/$6.99

It's always a challenge to find nearby points of interest, which is why I am so enamoured with Wikihood and Wikihood Plus. Chock-full of interesting facts about schools, museums, parks, churches, cities, historic locations, and much more, the app is also easy to use: You can either tap the compass button to find sights near your current location or use the search function to find sights near somewhere you're going. You can list places of interest by distance, relevance, or user rating, or you can view them as pins on a map. The Plus version offers two additional categories — economy and geography — plus more than 100,000 additional articles and the capability to search Wikipedia from within the app.

The World Clock
$0.99

My son spent last semester overseas, and I have friends and relatives in half a dozen countries around the world. The World Clock makes it easy for me to keep track of what time it is in all those places. It displays up to 24 clocks at a time — and it's easy to switch among three different clock types: two analogs and one digital. The app's built-in database knows almost 200,000 populated places in more than 230 countries, so it's very hard to stump. And it doesn't hurt that the app's day/night map and clocks are gorgeous. If you need to know the time in more than one place, look no further than The World Clock.

15 Utilities

1Password for iPad/ 1Password Pro

iPad only: $9.99; Pro (hybrid) $14.99

The desktop version of 1Password is a beautiful, elegant solution to the "too many passwords to remember" dilemma. I've used it for years on my Mac (a Windows beta is now available, too) and consider it one of a handful of must-have utilities. Now, 1Password for the iPad (and iPhone) is a must-have as well — and here's why:

I visit hundreds of Web sites regularly and many of them require my user name and password. Since I'm a firm believer in good Internet security, I like to use strong, unique passwords. So I don't use words from the dictionary or proper nouns. Instead, I use combinations of upper- and lowercase characters, symbols, and numerals, which makes my passwords difficult to guess. The problem is that such strong, unique passwords are nearly impossible for me to remember.

And that, folks, is just part of what I love about 1Password — it can open a Web page and then fill in the appropriate user name and password with just one tap of the finger. So, for example, when I want to log in to my Google account, I tap the arrow shown to the right of Google's URL in the figure on the left below. 1Password's built-in Web browser would then open the proper page and fill in my user name and password. While 1Password refers to this little trick as "Go & Fill," I just call it awesome.

The Go & Fill trick relies on 1Password's built-in Web browser, shown in the figure on the right below, because (at present) Apple doesn't allow third-party plug-ins for Safari on the iPad (or iPhone). It's a bare-bones Web browser with no bookmarks or history, but it's certainly usable in a pinch. If you do decide to use this built-in browser and you land on a page that requires you to log in, just tap the little globe icon at the top of the screen and then tap the login you want to use in the Logins over-lay (Google or YouTube in the figure on the right) — and watch your user name and password magically appear in the proper fields.

In addition to its awesome login trick, 1Password provides secure stor-age for other sensitive information such as account numbers, software licenses, and notes of any length.

1Password uses industry-standard 128-bit AES encryption. Every time you launch the app, you need to type the correct master password. Without it the app won't open, and then your data can't even be seen, much less used — thus it's completely protected should your iPad be stolen or misplaced.

If you own the desktop version of 1Password, you can synch over Wi-Fi or via Dropbox. And the desktop version has useful features you won't find in the current version of the iPad app — such as strong password generation and folders for organizing your logins.

Best features

Remembers all your user names and passwords and makes it easy to use them.

Worst features

Some cool features found in the 1Password desktop app are missing.

Atomic Web Browser
$0.99

The iPad's Safari Web browser doesn't suck (far from it), but the current version lacks several useful features available in Atomic Web Browser, including my favorites: tabbed browsing and full-screen browsing.

Let's start with tabbed browsing. As you know, Safari has only a reasonable facsimile of tabbed browsing: You can tap the double-square (multiple-pages) icon, as shown in the margin, which brings you to a separate screen that displays small versions of up to 9 pages. Atomic Web Browser, on the other hand, does tabbed browsing right, offering an unlimited number of real tabs, as shown in the figure on the left below.

Atomic Web Browser also offers some sweet tricks for working with tabs. For example, you can open up to eight bookmarks — each in its own tab — with a single tap if you so desire. And if you press and hold on a link (instead of just tapping it), an overlay asks whether you want to open the link into the existing tab, a new tab, or a new tab in the background.

My other favorite feature is full-screen browsing, shown in the figure on the right. The toolbar, bookmark bar, and tab bar disappear — so all you see is the Web site and a set of user-configurable translucent buttons at the bottom of the screen. I've tapped the + button in the figure on the right so you see the "Share" overlay in the middle of the screen. Notice that it offers several options you won't find in Safari — such as Post URL to Facebook or Twitter, and View Source (code).

Another feature you may find useful is Atomic Web Browser's Private Mode, which disables history and cookies when you enable it. You can also delete your history and cookies manually if you like. Plus, you can password-protect the Atomic Web Browser app itself so it can't be launched by anyone who doesn't know the password.

Another feature I like more and more is Atomic Web Browser's multi-touch gesture support. A two-fingered swipe left or right displays the previous tab or next tab, swipe up to see your home page, and swipe down to close the current tab. But the best gesture, at least in my humble opinion, is the three-fingered tap to enable/disable full-screen mode.

There's so much more that I don't know what features to leave out!

One feature I really appreciate is that I can search individual Web pages for a word or phrase. And speaking of searching, the search field in the toolbar gives you a choice of Amazon, Bing, eBay, Google, Wikipedia, Yahoo, or YouTube. Or you can install additional search-engine plug-ins with just two taps. Optional bookmark scripts add features such as the capability to translate a Web page to another language, track a UPS or FedEx package, or display the Google cache version of a Web page.

You can disable images if you need to (a very nice option if your Internet connection is pokey).

I don't much care for ad blockers (don't get me started), but Atomic Web Browser has one built in if you want it.

Best features

Tabbed and full-screen browsing are my personal favorites, though any of the features I mentioned could easily become yours.

Worst features

No way to import Safari (or Mac/PC) bookmarks.

 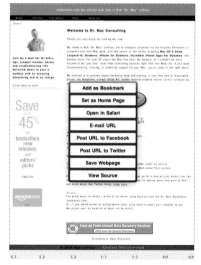

iTeleport
$24.99 US

iTeleport is one of the coolest and most useful apps I own — and by far the best app I've tried for remotely controlling my home or office computer. In other words, it lets me control computers running Mac, Windows, Linux, or AMX (another touch-screen operating system) from my iPad screen, no matter where in the world I might be.

If you've never used a VNC (Virtual Network Computing, sometimes called *screen-sharing*) program to control your computer remotely, here's how it works: When you run iTeleport, you see the remote computer's screen and control its mouse pointer and keyboard with your iPad. To prepare a computer for this type of remote control, you first install software called a *VNC server*. For iTeleport, you download the free server software from the iTeleport Web site. As long as the computer has an Internet connection and is running the VNC server software, you can use a user name and password to connect to and control the computer from iTeleport on your iPad (or iPhone — it's a hybrid) — from anywhere in the world.

If you've never tried remote-control computing, it's fabulous — and often a lifesaver. iTeleport has saved my bacon more times than I care to remember. For example, I can use iTeleport on my iPad or iPhone to look at the e-mail in the Inbox of my desktop computer back at the office, as shown in the figure on the left. If there's an urgent message in my Inbox, I can reply to it remotely, as I did in the figure on the left. Or I can forward it to my iPad (which has a separate e-mail address) and deal with it from there.

I've been known to use iTeleport to look up a recipe on my home computer while I'm out shopping. Finally, if I'm out and about and someone needs a document from my Mac, I can use iTeleport to e-mail the document, even if I'm on the other side of the world. And that's just what I'm doing in the figure on the right below.

iTeleport has full keyboard support, so you can use it to type text into any app running on your remote computer. It also supports all modifier keys such as those shown (left to right) near the top of the figure on the right: Shift, Control, ⌘, and Option. And there are lots of shortcut buttons for common activities such as quit (an application), close (a window), switch (applications), select all, cut, copy, and paste — all of which are shown at the bottom of the figure on the right.

I've tried similar VNC client apps that claim to do what iTeleport does, but none have worked as well or as reliably.

Best features

iTeleport lets me be at my computer even when I'm nowhere near it. If there's something I need from my home or office Mac, iTeleport lets me access it from wherever I happen to be. This app may seem expensive to you, but to me it's easily worth every cent.

Worst features

I use two displays at home, but iTeleport can only access the main one (the one with the menu bar). Consequently, I have to make sure I don't leave windows or icons on the secondary display if I might need to use them via iTeleport.

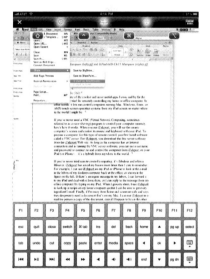

Lifelike Alarm Clock and Weather HD
$3.99

Although the iPhone includes a decent enough Clock app that includes multiple alarms and world clocks, plus a timer and a stopwatch, the iPad includes bupkis in the clock department. So if you desire clock functionality, you'll need an app for that. Fortunately, there's no shortage of such apps.

That's the good news. The bad news is that, at least for now, none of the iPad alarm clocks will run in the background like the iPhone clock. So the app has to be running; if it isn't, your alarms will never be heard. I suspect this will be resolved when iOS4 becomes available for the iPad and the app developers update their apps to take advantage of its multitasking function. But for now, any alarm clock app on your iPad has to be open if you want to hear its alarms.

That said, I looked at close to a dozen alarm clocks for the iPad. Some were more expensive, others were less expensive, and several were free. But at the end of the day (I don't know about you, but that's when I need an alarm clock), the one I liked best was this one.

There are a lot of apps with "clock" and/or "weather" in their names; the one I recommend here is called *Lifelike Alarm Clock and Weather HD*.

There are many things I like about this app. Let me start with the vital (to me) functionality. Unlike some other clock apps I've tested, it's incredibly easy to use. You won't need a manual or instructions; everything works just as you expect. More specifically, it's very easy to set new alarms, and it's easy to choose a song or songs to use as alarms.

I told you I was a bit of a weather nut in Chapter 14 — I really like seeing the weather forecast before I even get out of bed. And I like being able to tap the + button for additional details, as shown in the figure on the right below.

I don't use a sleep timer at home, but when I'm on the road, I appreciate falling asleep to one of the included relaxation sounds, as shown in the figure on the left below. Or, if I prefer, I can fall asleep to my choice of songs from my library.

Notice the little windowshade pull in the upper-left corner of both figures below? Pull it downward and the app goes into the best nighttime
display mode I've seen so far. When invoked, the screen turns black and
displays the time and current temperature in very, very dim gray. But if
that's too dark for you, there's a manual brightness control as well.

Finally, when an alarm goes off, the screen that appears is near-perfect,
displaying huge on-screen buttons that let you turn off the alarm completely or snooze for 5, 10, 20, or 30 minutes, with a single tap.

I also like the look and feel of this app. I think the five included clocks —
two analog and three digital — are as pretty as on-screen clocks get, and
I love the cool rotary volume control.

Best features

Great design and ease of use are what make this app stand out in a
crowded field.

Worst features

Unlike the iPhone clock app, it has no timer or stopwatch. Bummer!

Marquee
$1.99

There's no shortage of apps that turn your iPad into a mobile sign or moving banner — I counted at least half a dozen today, and by the time you read this there will no doubt be many more. Marquee isn't the cheapest but it does provide the most bang for your buck (actually the most bang for your *two* bucks), with more options and choices than any other app I tested.

The first time you use Marquee you'll see a list containing 16 sample messages, as shown in the figure on the left below. You can use them, modify them, or even delete them if you like.

If you tapped the Groups button in the upper-left corner of the screen you'd discover that these 16 messages belong to the group called "Marquee." So you can create your own groups, which can contain only your own messages, or you could create new messages in the Marquee group by tapping the + sign at the bottom-right corner of the screen.

These groups serve a unique and useful function in addition to helping you organize your messages; you can tap the Play button (bottom-center in the figure on the left) to play all messages in the current group (Marquee). This is a powerful feature — and one I didn't see in any of the other apps I tried.

Of course, you can tap any message to display it on the screen; it will appear in the orientation your iPad is in. Or you can use one of Marquee's global settings to lock your iPad into either portrait or land-scape mode. Other global settings include an optional alert after the last message in a group appears, a time limit so you don't run down your battery, and the length of the delay between messages.

To edit an existing message, you tap the blue detail disclosure button on its right to display the message's Edit Message screen, as shown in the figure on the right below.

Along the top of the Edit Message screen are five icons; tap them to insert (from left to right) current time, current date, song currently playing in your iPad's iPod app (if any), picture from your Photos app (great for adding things such as your company's logo), and high-resolution emoticons (that is, smileys). You have a choice of 17 fonts and a myriad of background and font colors. And you can set the scrolling speed of each message from extremely slow (turtle icon) to very fast (rabbit icon).

Marquee Styles are another nice touch. In addition to the usual banner effect that scrolls text from left to right, you can also scroll in reverse for Arabic or Hebrew messages. Other styles include two different zoom effects that enlarge your text as it blasts onto the screen, and a pair of elegant-looking fade-in/fade-out effects.

If all you need is a simple scrolling banner, search the App Store for "billboard" or "banner," and grab one of the freebies. But if you want to create great-looking signs, get Marquee.

Best features

The best thing about Marquee is that you have lots of options, which means you can be more creative with your banners and scrolling signs than with most other apps. The high-res smileys and the capability to include photos are also quite nice.

Worst features

There aren't enough emoticons — only about 30 of 'em. I'd sure love to see more.

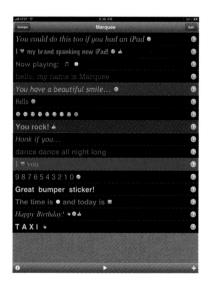

Air Display
$9.99

Ever wish your computer screen were a wee bit bigger? Well, with Air Display, your iPad turns into a wireless extension of your Mac or PC screen, giving you an additional 1,024 x 768 pixels of screen real estate. It's a great place to park windows or palettes you don't need on your main screen — and it works great. Just download and install the free Air Display server software on your computer, fire up the Air Display app on your iPad, and presto — you have another computer display screen! And at $10 it's a heck of a lot cheaper than even the cheapest flat-screen display.

Air Sharing HD
$9.99

From the same brilliant developers who created Air Display, Air Sharing HD turns your iPad into a wireless hard disk, making it an easier way (than iTunes) to get your files onto your iPad. Your Mac, PC, or Linux computer mounts the iPad as it would any network disk — and you can then view, e-mail, or print the files residing on it. (Sadly, printing is Mac- and Linux-only, so Windows users are out of luck.) And you can browse the contents of .ZIP archives on your iPad without unzipping them! You can even share documents with other Air Sharing users on the same Wi-Fi network.

Audio Memos Free — The Voice Recorder
Free

The iPhone comes with a voice-recorder app but the iPad doesn't. Now I've got a dozen or more apps that can record audio memos, but Audio Memos Free — The Voice Recorder does everything you're likely to need (and more) — for free. You can send your recordings (up to 3MB) via e-mail, choose from three levels of recording quality, apply normalization and/or level boost to minimize distortion and clipping, and take advantage of a built-in server for getting your audio files onto your Mac or PC from the iPad. If that's not enough, there are two paid versions of this app — one for $0.99 and one for $4.99 — that add numerous features.

Calculator XL
Free

The Calculator is another useful app that you get free with the iPhone but not with the iPad. And while I rarely use a calculator (I'm all about letting a spreadsheet do the math for me), the one I use when I have to use one on my iPad is Calculator XL. It's free and it includes all the functions I'm likely to need — addition, subtraction, multiplication, and division — plus memory. And it retains its memory even after you quit the app. Check out the $0.99 in-app upgrade to add an easy tip calculator, conversion calculator, and more.

Free App Tracker
Free

I'm going to go out on a limb here and assume you're a person who enjoys iPad apps. And if you're anything like me, you also like to find bargains — or, better still, free stuff. If any or all of that is true, you'll love the Free App Tracker app. It shows you apps that have had their prices reduced, apps that have gone from paid to free, and the most popular free apps. Plus, if there's a paid app you want but you don't want to pay its current price, the app can track it and inform you if its price goes down.

16 Miscellaneous

Bryan's Top Ten Apps

- Air Sketch
- Isaac Newton's Gravity HD
- Kingdom of the Blue Whale iPad HD
- Stair Dismount Universal
- TextExpander
- At Bat 2010 for iPad
- Chronicle for iPad — A Personal Journal
- My Writing Nook for iPad
- Parallels Mobile
- Seline HD — Musical Instrument

Air Sketch
$5.99

There are several sketching and whiteboard apps for the iPad, but Air Sketch offers a great feature that sets it apart: You can share your sketching and whiteboard sessions over a network. Anyone with a computer and a browser who's on your network can follow along while you sketch, write, or go from slide to slide.

It works like this: Included in the app is a sort of mini-Web server. In the figure below, I've tapped the icon in the lower-right corner of the screen. The pop-up window includes the IP address that your viewers would plug into their browsers. In my case, that address is

```
http://10.0.1.23:8080
```

Your viewers would simply put that address in the URL field of any HTML 5-compliant browser (Safari or Firefox are recommended), and they'll see whatever you're doing in Air Sketch! It's very easy to use, even for non-techies.

 Air Sketch is technically recommended for sharing to just one computer, but I was able to share it successfully to two computers and an iPhone without any trouble.

You can use the app as a blank whiteboard, but you can also pull up images from your photo library. If you've preloaded your slides, for instance, you could use Air Sketch as a nifty presentation tool — and interact with those slides in real time. As an example, the figure below is a slide I originally created in Keynote.

Let's take that handy feature one step further and use a computer that's connected to a projector. Now you can use Air Sketch to deliver your presentation to a large room full of people without chaining yourself to a podium! Clever uses like this are how the iPad is going to change the way we do a lot of things.

There aren't any text or shape tools in this app. Instead, you have five pen tools (pencil, pen, felt-tip, paint brush, and a highlighter). There are also eight color swatches, as you can see in the figure below, each of which can be customized with a double-tap. There's also an eraser, undo and redo, and the capability to save screen captures to your photo library with one tap. You can also e-mail one of your sketches as a PDF or as an image file.

You can pinch and zoom in on your sketches on your iPad, while the image stays full-screen for your viewers. This is handy for making smaller text or drawings.

I recommend a stylus like the Pogo Sketch Stylus for writing and sketching. The fact that you don't need a stylus to use the iPad is great, but a pen still makes for better handwritten text.

There's a free version of the app that allows you to sketch and test the networking functions, so try it if you aren't sure you need this app.

Best features

The capability to share your sessions with others on the same network makes this an awesome sketching and whiteboard app!

Worst features

There are no text or shape tools, both of which would drastically increase this app's functionality.

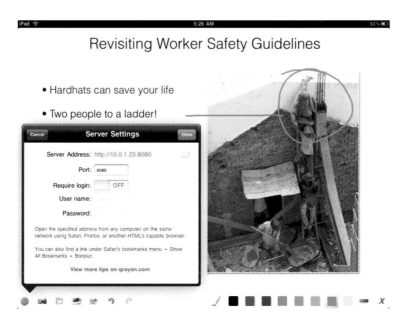

Isaac Newton's Gravity HD
Free ($9.99)

Don't tell Bob, but I'm sneaking a game into this chapter. He got to cover all the games back in Chapter 7, but I'm using the excuse that this game has the word "gravity" in it to slip it in here! Which is cool, because this is one of my favorite time-sinks on the iPad. It combines a fun concept, great graphics, and really hard physics-based puzzles into a mental workout that has so much "just one more level" appeal that you'll wonder where your day went.

The central premise of this game is that for each level there's a button that simply has to be pushed; to push it, you have a ball. The problem, of course, is that there's no direct path from where the ball starts to where the button sits in all its red, "push me, please" goodness. To help bridge the gaps, pits, traps, and other roadblocks, the player gets blocks, levers, marbles, and rolling eyeballs that you then use to find a solution. Every level gets different objects, and not every tool is always required on each map. In addition, there is often (and maybe even always — you'd have to ask someone mathier than me) more than one solution for each level.

In the figure below, I'm pretty sure I can bounce the ball off the pi-shaped structure and then off the top of the other object that has the gear around it. A single tap selects an object; you can then use the gear to drag it around or to spin it 360 degrees until it's positioned the way you want it.

Try to think differently about each level: You don't always have to use the main ball to push the button. Sometimes you can throw, bump, bounce, or push some of your other objects into the button, instead!

The game has a built-in hint system, but the developers were really evil about how they set it up. You get some 300 points to spend on hints, and the higher the level, the more expensive the hint, so spend your hint-points wisely. There's also a Trophy Room with different awards for completing levels without using a hint, for solving a level after many tries, and more.

I've marked the price as Free with $9.99 in parentheses because the game is ostensibly a free download, and for that price you get eight levels. For $9.99 you can make an in-app purchase for the other 92 levels — for a total of 100 levels of gravity goodness. If you can resist making that purchase after playing eight levels, you're made of sterner stuff than I am!

In addition to the 100 levels included with in-app purchase, you can also create your own levels or download levels that other users have created. As of this writing, there are close to a thousand user-created levels — and the library is growing all the time.

Bob adds: I'm glad you "snuck" this one in. On the other hand, I keep playing, "one more level," so I'm not doing something I should be doing. Great app, Bryan. I could have done without another amazing time-sucker, but I'm glad you included it.

Best features

Super fun, very challenging, great graphics, and physics! Plus, the "just one more" factor will drive you to distraction, but in a good way.

Worst features

Sometimes the pieces get stuck, and it becomes hard to move them around. This can particularly so on levels with a lot going on in them. At $9.99, the in-app purchase for the full game is a little on the expensive side.

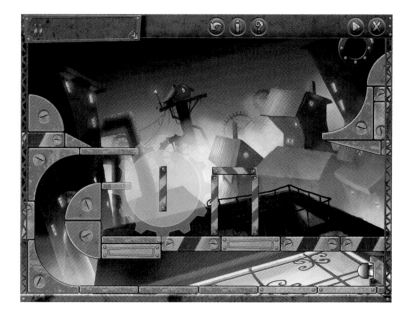

Kingdom of the Blue Whale iPad HD

$2.99

This title was released the day I wrote this chapter, and I'm glad it came out in time to be included in the book because it's a really cool app! The laboriously named Kingdom of the Blue Whale iPad HD from National Geographic (Nat Geo) turns some awesome-looking ocean photography into a jigsaw puzzle. And it turns out that the iPad is a great medium for puzzles! Who knew?

Kingdom of the Blue Whale iPad HD comes with 50 photos from Nat Geo's archives, all of them related to the ocean, and many of them involving whales. You can take those photos and turn them into puzzles, but you can also share them to Facebook, e-mail them, or save them to your photo library for use as wallpaper for your iPad.

You can also turn any photo in your library into a puzzle. You'll see a Personal option when you tap New Game that you can use to browse your photo library.

As I mentioned above, I was surprised at how much fun it was to put a puzzle together on my iPad. The developers who made the game for Nat Geo did a fine job of using iPad conventions to turn your display into a great workspace for moving puzzle pieces around and putting them together. For one thing, the workspace is larger than the display itself. If you tap and drag a piece, you move the piece. If you tap and drag a blank part of the screen, you move the whole workspace. That means you can move individual pieces (or maybe all the pieces you've assembled so far) aside, giving you plenty of room to work. When you find two pieces that go together, just move them so the two sides that connect are touching and they'll snick together on their own.

In the figure below, you'll see a timer in the upper-right corner of the screen. This is a nice feature for those who like to challenge themselves, although the app has no scoreboard.

There are four difficulty levels for each puzzle: Easy (2x3), Medium (4x5), Hard (5x6), and Expert (6x7). In the figure below, you'll see a puzzle on the Expert setting with 42 pieces. (That's not very expert, in my opinion, though it's still fun.) And because there are four difficulty levels for each image, even young kids can have fun with this app;

adults will enjoy a casual puzzle session. And if you have to stop working on a puzzle, you can pick it up where you left off. Try that with a real puzzle on your kitchen table!

There are two kinds of puzzle shapes: Classic and Elegant. I'm using the Classic shape in the puzzle below.

You can also just browse the gallery of 50 images. Nat Geo is, of course, known for its photography, and these are some really beautiful images.

Lastly, the app uses the multitouch capabilities of the iPad to allow multiple people to work on a puzzle at one time! That's pretty slick, in my book!

Best features

Nat Geo has made it super easy to put a puzzle together, and it's really fun. Plus: You can't lose the pieces, and there's no cleanup afterwards!

Worst features

All the puzzle pieces are aligned properly — I want an option to scramble even that. Also, Expert difficulty is only 6x7 pieces. I'd like to see something a couple of orders of magnitude harder. Come on, it's an iPad!

Stair Dismount Universal
Free

This innocuously named game is super fun, but I won't be offended if you find it deplorable. In fact, just skip ahead to the next incredible iPad app if you abhor violence or have a little good taste.

Okay, now that we ditched the goody-two-shoes crowd, the rest of us can enjoy this guilty pleasure of a game! Stair Dismount Universal is part 3D physics emulator and part awful. The point of the game is to watch what happens when you push Mr. Dismount, a test dummy ragdoll, down a flight of stairs. No, I'm serious, that's the point of the game, and you get points according to how much damage you do to the ragdoll, with bonus points for somersaults achieved during the fall. As he falls, his ragdoll body lights up in orange where it gets damaged — the greater the damage, the brighter the orange.

It sounds just awful, doesn't it? The worst thing is the sound your ragdoll makes as it tumbles down the stairs. It's this horrible, twig breaking sound, but you can turn the effects volume down in the settings.

So why would I cover such an awful game? Because it's fun! To play, you first pick a ragdoll. The game is free, and you get one ragdoll, the above-mentioned Mr. Dismount, included for that price. There are also three more ragdoll types you can buy through an in-app purchase for $0.99 each. When you choose your ragdoll, you can choose to put a photo on the face, using photos from your iPad's library, or from Facebook. Then you choose from 1 of 12 different levels, each with its own stair or other platform.

Your ragdoll will then be perched at the top of the stairs, waiting for a push. You can choose where you push him by dragging your finger across his body. This is a fully 3D world, so you can drag the camera to any direction you want, and you can push Mr. Dismount from any direction, too. There is a power meter at the bottom of the screen that allows you to choose how hard you push, and that's the modicum of intellectual legitimacy to the game, because now you get to truly experiment with the effects of gravity and force, all in a virtual setting!

In the figure to the left below, I'm about to introduce Mr. Dismount to mean ol' Dr. Gravity. The circle and arrow on his back mark the spot where I'm going to push him. In the figure to the right below, Mr. Dismount is kindly showing us what happens to you when you hit a crossbeam on your way down.

The game keeps track of high scores for each level, and it supports OpenFeint, the multiplayer service for iOS games. It also offers replays of the most recent fall, and it will take a screenshot that looks a lot like a crime-scene investigation photo that you can save, e-mail, or post on Facebook. There's also a scoring page for each fall that details the damage taken by your ragdoll.

Best features

It's terribly fun, and it has what seems to me to be a very accurate physics engine (combined with a macabre sense of humor, of course). I suspect you'll play this game far longer than you'll admit to strangers.

Worst features

You're pushing someone off a set of stairs! Come on, people, what's wrong with you?

TextExpander
$4.99

TextExpander is one of those apps you'll wonder how you did without once you start using it. With this app, you can set up short codes that TextExpander then expands automatically into a full word or phrase. It's perfect for those things that we type over and over again — signature lines, addresses, phone numbers, code snippets, greetings, and other repetitive phrases. When you get used to using the abbreviation you set up, your wrists will thank you. Long a staple on the Mac platform, SmileSoftware TextExpander has come to the iPad (and iPhone), and that makes me pretty happy!

On your Mac, TextExpander runs in the background, always watching what you're typing, ready to jump in and do its thing. That's not possible on iOS, not even iOS 4.x with its limited ability to run more than one app at a time. Apps not in the foreground are in stasis; they can't actually do anything when they're in the background.

iOS 4 brought background apps to the iPhone 4G when it was released in June 2010. The release date for the iPad version of this feature is November 2010.

The smart folks at Smile attacked this issue of background apps in two ways:

- ✔ **You can type up notes from within the TextExpander app itself, then copy them to your clipboard and paste them from the app you actually need the text in.** For instance, you can compose an e-mail in TextExpander, and then send it to your Mail app.

- ✔ **Smile has released an API that other iOS apps developers can add into their apps that makes them "TextExpander-aware."** This approach is extra-cool: Currently about 40 apps have this feature (and some of them are featured in this book, so they *must* be cool!). If an app is TextExpander-aware, it taps into your TextExpander database of snippets and does the substitution for you — simple as that. As long as you have TextExpander installed on your iPad, those apps just do that TextExpander thing automatically.

Use codes for the snippets you aren't likely to use by accident. For instance, instead of add for your address, use aaddr (so you don't trigger your whole address when you type the word *add*).You can also put a number in your code, such as sig1 or sms1, so that the letters alone don't trigger the substitution.

It's hard to show you a screenshot of the substitution itself because it's so seamless. One second you have all but one letter or number of your code, and the next it's been auto-expanded. Instead, I have a screenshot of some of the snippets on my iPad, as you can see in the figure below.

You can organize your snippets into groups to make it easier to manage them. If you have a lot of snippets, you should absolutely use this feature!

Lastly, you can send your snippets from your iPad to another iOS device (that has TextExpander installed), or you can load snippets from that device to your iPad. If you use TextExpander on your Mac, you can do the same thing.

Best features

I love that other apps can add support for TextExpander, and I hope to see many more developers do so in the future. Also, the app is intuitive and easy to use.

Worst features

Not every app is TextExpander-aware, and some great apps — notably Apple's Mail app or its AppleWorks suite — are unlikely ever to add this feature.

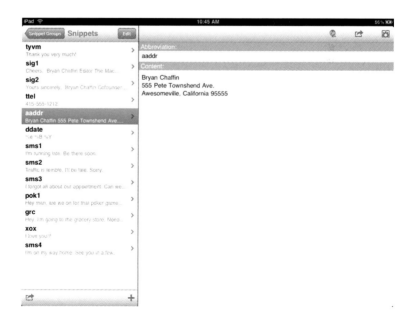

At Bat 2010 for iPad
$6.99 (limited offer)

Baseball nuts have simply got to get this app for their iPads. Put out by Major League Baseball, this app gives you player stats, pitching information (you can track the location, speed, and type of pitch for every pitch thrown in an MLB game, for goodness sake!), and live audio broadcasts of games. And if you subscribe to MLB.tv, you can watch live games through the app, too. There's a lot of content in this app.

MLB releases a new app for every season, so simply look for the current season when you're looking for it in iTunes.

Chronicle for iPad — A Personal Journal
$1.99

It seems to me that the iPad could be the perfect device for a personal journal, which may be why there are lots of journal apps for the iPad on the App Store. Chronicle for iPad is the best of the ones I looked at, and it offers lots of features so you can make the kind of journal you want. You can customize the background color, add photos from your photo library, search text, or view in calendar mode. You can type in portrait or landscape mode, export the journal as a PDF file — or straight to Google Docs — or put a password on it to give it some extra protection above and beyond the iPad's security feature.

My Writing Nook for iPad
$4.99

My Writing Nook for iPad is a nice app for creative writing, for a couple of reasons. For one thing, it fully supports external keyboards. For another, the app has a browser-based companion service that runs on Google App Engine. You can save your documents to the online service, and edit them from any browser. When you're working on your iPad, the app offers word count, font controls, and support for TextExpander Touch, which I wrote about earlier in this chapter. It will autosave your documents and auto spell-check them, and you can organize your documents into groups. It also features an app-based passcode for extra security.

Parallels Mobile
Free

This app is a companion app for Parallels Desktop, the virtual-machine software that allows you to run Windows on your Mac. With Parallels Mobile, you can actually pull up the instance of Parallels that's running on your Mac — from your iPad — which means you can use Windows apps on your iPad too! The company even implemented specific gestures to emulate all the Windows mouse clicks. Note that Parallels Mobile is a free download, but it's useless without Parallels ($79.99) *and* Windows ($119.99 and up). Also, Bob covered an app in Chapter 15 — iTeleport ($24.99) — that gives you direct access to any computer running that app, but if all you need to do is access Parallels remotely, this free app is a great choice.

Seline HD — Musical Instrument
$9.99

Seline HD is a cool music app, but it was released after Bob wrote Chapter 9 (the music chapter), so he asked me to include it here. It's a fun app, and I was happy to comply! Seline HD is one of the first musical-instrument apps that approaches the iPad as a completely new medium for music. It uses an interface called ioGrid that was designed from the ground up for the iPad — in other words, this isn't a digital conversion of an analog instrument. The app generates droning backing tracks while you play melodies, and it has two effects, twenty main instrument voices (plus nine drone voices), and you can record what you play!

17 Ten Favorite Free Apps

Bob's Top Ten Free Apps

▷ Comics

▷ Dragon Dictation

▷ Dropbox

▷ Epicurious Recipes & Shopping List

▷ Flipboard

▷ Google Mobile App

▷ iBooks

▷ Pandora Radio

▷ Pocket Legends

▷ Shazam for iPad

 ## Comics
Free

If you read what I had to say in Chapter 2, you already know that I love this app. My biggest gripe was that the app didn't have enough comics from "the big guys" (such as Marvel and DC Comics). But things seem to be improving: The app now has hundreds of titles from Marvel and DC Comics, with more added almost every week.

I also talk about Guided View in Chapter 2. I only wish this book had video — because you have to see Guided View in motion (as opposed to the still simulation I attempted in Chapter 2) to appreciate it.

The bottom line

If you like comics or graphic novels, you're sure to enjoy this app.

Dragon Dictation
Free

If I've got a lot of text to input on my iPad I generally turn to Dragon Dictation. I use this app to knock out a first draft — and how well its speech-recognition engine works almost always impresses me.

Unfortunately, I find that *editing* text using my iPad's onscreen keyboard is even more painful than *typing* text with it, so here are two things that help me avoid editing long documents:

- ✔ My favorite trick is to e-mail the text to myself — which Dragon Dictate lets me do with a couple of taps, as shown in the figure below — and then I edit the text on my desktop or laptop computer. Once the piece is properly polished on my computer I can do whatever I need to do with it, such as print it, save it in a different file format, or use the finished document on my iPad via either iTunes File Sharing or by e-mailing it to my iPad.

- ✔ My second-favorite trick is to use my Apple Wireless Keyboard (see Chapter 19) for text editing on my iPad.

The bottom line

Dragon Dictation should have been bundled with the iPad. Yes, it's that good.

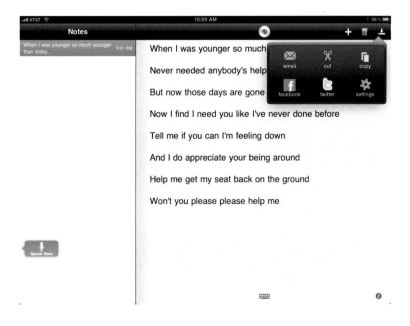

Dropbox
Free

So here's the deal: I think Dropbox is fantastic for many reasons, but the big one is that it lets me synchronize documents among my desktop computer, my notebook computer, my iPad, my iPhone, and even the cloud. That cloud part means, in addition to having the most recent version of important documents available on all my electronic devices, I can also access those documents with any Web browser — on any Web-connected computer — in any location on Earth that has Internet access.

Even if you use another backup solution, having redundant backups in multiple physical locations is an excellent idea.

Dropbox comes with 2GB of free online storage. That may be enough for you but it wasn't enough for me. So I took advantage of the Dropbox "tell-a-friend" offer and told my friends how much I like Dropbox. If they decide to create free accounts, I receive a free 250MB of storage — up to 8GB. So, since I had 32 friends who signed up, I now have 10GB of free Dropbox storage.

The bottom line

Almost all of the 32 friends who signed up love Dropbox. And you're going to love it, too.

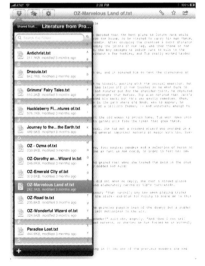

Epicurious Recipes & Shopping List

Free (Ad-Supported)

I love to cook and I love to shop for food — so the Epicurious Recipes & Shopping List app is one of my all-time faves at any price. And since it was Bryan who told you all about it in Chapter 6, I'll tell you why I love it in a moment. But first, a bit of background . . . .

Over the past few years, I've typed, scanned, bookmarked, or created PDF files of hundreds of my favorite recipes. I store them all in a folder I call (d'oh!) Recipes, which resides inside the Dropbox folder on my Mac's hard drive. This way, if I need to plan or shop for a meal while I'm out and about, my recipe files are available via the Dropbox app on my iPad or iPhone.

But when I don't know what I want to cook, or I want to try cooking something different, Epicurious is usually the only app I need.

The bottom line

As Bryan indicated in Chapter 6, the Epicurious app is well designed, cleverly programmed, and truly a pleasure to use.

Flipboard
Free

Bryan raved and raved about Flipboard in Chapter 10, so I had to check it out. And guess what, folks? Bryan is spot-on. I really, really like Flipboard. I like how it displays "articles" from my Facebook wall better than I like the way Facebook itself displays items on my wall in a Web browser. In fact, I enjoy reading stories on my Facebook wall with Flipboard much more than I enjoy reading them using any Web browser on any platform or device.

As for Twitter, I think the way Flipboard presents my Twitter feed is brilliant. This, too, is much more watchable than the scrolling list of all-text tweets you find on the Twitter Web site and most Twitter clients.

 Bryan's review of Flipboard in Chapter 10 included a picture (the one on the left) of a Twitter feed. If you're wondering why most of the articles in that figure contain more than 140 characters — the maximum length of a tweet — it's because Flipboard shows you interesting articles that were *mentioned* in someone's tweet; the tweeter's name appears with a "Shared by" credit.

The bottom line
What have you got to lose? Try it; it's free.

Google Mobile App

Free

Bryan gushed about this app in Chapter 12 so let me tell you a couple of the reasons *I* love this app too:

✔ **Reason #1:** Its speech-to-text engine is amazingly accurate. I've tried many speech-to-text systems over the years. Google Mobile is right up there with the best.

✔ **Reason #2:** If you meet someone who asks how your iPad works, demonstrate it by pulling yours out, launching Google Mobile, and asking it to search for something on the Web. Then hand it to the person and watch their jaw drop when they see the search results on the screen. Not many apps work as well for an iPad demo, and that's priceless.

Tap the magnifying glass on the left side of the Search field to narrow your search, as shown in both pictures below. When I selected Images, then spoke the words "Vizsla dog," Google Mobile understood perfectly and displayed the results you see on the left below. When I selected Shopping and spoke the words, "Logitech Performance Mouse MX," Google Mobile not only got the words right, but the search results were just what I had hoped for, shown in the figure on the right below.

The bottom line

Searching the Web with Google Mobile is better, easier, and more fun than using Safari.

iBooks

Free

I told you about the iBooks app way back in Chapter 2, but I didn't show you any pictures. I'll rectify that here.

For what it's worth, that was one of the hardest parts of writing this book — figuring out which apps get screen shots and which apps don't.

In the figure on the left, I'm reading *Winnie-the-Pooh*. The brightness, font, search, and bookmark controls appear in the top-right corner, and the page selector control (with preview) is down at the bottom.

I'm cheap. So I like the iBooks Store's substantial selection of free books and free previews of paid books. In the figure on the right below, I've downloaded five of the top eight free books (and many more). At the bottom of the screen are the iBooks Store five tabs — Featured, NYTimes, Top Charts, Browse, and Purchases. Also notice the overlay on the left side of the screen, which lets you browse various categories.

The bottom line

It's free — and there's a lot of good reading material that's free, too. Even if that's all you ever use it for, you really ought to check it out. An i-book might be just the ticket next time you and your iPad have a few minutes of downtime.

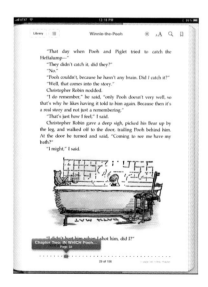

Pandora Radio
Free

I gushed about Pandora in Chapter 9, but that's because I love it. It's the best thing I've ever heard when it comes to discovering new music I'm likely to like.

The reason Pandora works so well is the Music Genome Project. It consists of hundreds of musical attributes, or *genes,* that together capture the unique and magical essence of a song — its melody, harmony, rhythm, instrumentation, orchestration, arrangement, lyrics, singing, and vocal harmony.

I prefer to create my Pandora radio stations with a Web browser on my desktop computer (rather than with this app). You have more control over a radio station's "seed" content on the Web.

When you give a song thumbs-up or thumbs-down by tapping the appropriate icon, you help Pandora learn your tastes and pick songs you're even more likely to enjoy. The more you listen (and rate songs by tapping the thumbs-up and -down icons), the better Pandora gets to know your musical preferences.

The bottom line

Want to hear new music you're almost certain to enjoy? Get Pandora Radio.

Pocket Legends
Free

When last we spoke about Pocket Legends (which was in Chapter 7, to be precise), my parting words were a mini-rant about how difficult it was to zoom in on the action and enjoy the terrific graphics and fine details without dying a thousand horrible deaths.

And so, gentle reader, I took it upon myself to practice killing zombies and other nasties while zoomed in as far as possible. Why? So I could live long enough to get an awesome screen shot for you, like the one below.

In this figure I'm Doc, the birdlike guy with his back to the camera and a lightning-spewing stick in his claws. A dotted line extends from Doc to the little zombie dude. His health is around 69%, as reported by the little red bar above his head. He's a goner and I'll dispatch him before he even gets close. Then I'll have to kill the other zombies lumbering near the top of the screen.

The bottom line

It's free, fun, and ever-evolving.

Shazam for iPad
Free

What Shazam does sounds like magic to my ears. If you recall, in Chapter 9, I told you I tried my best to stump Shazam, but it named almost every tune I played for it, no matter how obscure.

I tried to stump it again before I started this chapter. Shazam nailed even the most obscure artists and songs by the likes of John Coltrane, Miles Davis, Buddy Guy, Taj Mahal, Rufus Wainwright, Jackson Browne & David Lindley, Infant Sorrow, Eddie Vedder, and Dave Brubeck. It even identified random sections of Emerson, Lake & Palmer's 20-minute opus, "Tarkus."

This go-round Shazam was only stumped by some obscure Art Farmer tracks.

Just trust me — for popular music from the last 60 or 70 years, it's pretty incredible.

Okay, now that that's settled, here's how Shazam has worked for me. The other day I heard a song. I knew I liked it but couldn't recall the artist or song title. Shazam knew the title, artist, and more in mere seconds. That led me to check out the artist info, shown in the figure on the left below.

The bottom line
Shazam can probably name that tune even if you can't.

18 Ten Favorite Paid Apps

Bob's Top Ten Apps

▷ 1Password

▷ Air Display

▷ Air Video

▷ Angry Birds

▷ Bill Atkinson's PhotoCard

▷ Atomic Web Browser

▷ Improvox

▷ Instapaper

▷ iTeleport

▷ OmniGraffle

1Password
iPad only: $9.99;
Pro (hybrid) $14.99

I have more than 500 different logins stored in my 1Password database. Even if the majority of them were for sites and services I no longer use (which they're not), 1Password would still remember my login name and password for hundreds of sites, apps, wireless networks, and other services.

For example, I open 1Password on my iPad and tap Amazon.com in my Logins list, as shown in the figure on the left below. The built-in 1Password Web browser opens to Amazon.com and I'm already logged in to my account.

The bottom line

Having all of my user names and passwords synchronized and available on my iPad, iPhone, and both of my computers is pure bliss.

Air Display
$9.99

I was working on my laptop, reviewing screen shots for the apps in this chapter. I was, of course, using Air Display, so I captured the moment in the figure you see below. What you're seeing is my iPad screen, with this chapter and the Dummies Styles palette. On my computer's main screen (not shown) are several images I'm considering for use with this chapter.

Having the Word file on a second screen — my iPad screen courtesy of the Air Display app — really streamlines my workflow. Without it, I'd have to show and hide the Word document or move it around onscreen almost constantly.

I also like programs with palettes or toolboxes. I move the tools onto the iPad screen and use the main computer screen to focus on the project at hand. It's great for apps like Photoshop, PowerPoint, and Keynote, to name a few that benefit from the additional screen real estate.

The bottom line

Think of Air Display as a second screen for your laptop or desktop computer that costs less than $10.

Air Video
$2.99

At this writing, the iPad has either 32 or 64GB of storage. A maximum of 64GB for all of your apps, music, movies, TV shows, photos, podcasts, audiobooks, and everything else.

Therein lies the rub. I have around 200GB of movies and TV shows on my hard drives at home. Even if I didn't have any apps, music, photos, or other data, I could only have 25 percent of my video collection on the iPad at any time.

I, for example, have over 100 episodes (25GB) of *Family Guy*. I'm not proud . . . it's one of my guilty pleasures. I never know which episode I'll want to watch or which ones my friend(s) may not have seen.

I've tried other apps that claim to stream your videos from home, but none of them worked as well as Air Video. And the app handles conversion behind the scenes, so no matter what format the original video is stored in you can watch it now on the iPad, as shown in the figure below. Or add the movie to the queue and let your computer process it for improved viewing later.

The bottom line

If you have lots of video and want to watch any or all of it on your iPad, Air Video is a steal at $2.99.

Angry Birds
$4.99

Both of my kids tell me that everyone they know with an iPhone plays Angry Birds and loves it. And I agree that the $0.99 iPhone version totally rocks. But the game is SO much more fun on an iPad it's not funny.

Actually, it *is* funny and at the same time, not so much. Some of the dorky levels and dumb-looking birds make me laugh out loud. And don't mute the sound — these birds make great noises when they splatter. On the other hand, some of the more insidious levels make me want to cry.

I'm one level away from finishing the last level on the iPad and I can't bring myself to actually do it. I'm afraid I'll have Angry Birds withdrawal.

Fortunately, the developer has added new content several times via free app updates, so I hold out hope that there will be additional levels for the iPad version soon.

The bottom line

I don't know what else to say about it. It's stupid, it's dorky, and I can't stop playing it.

Bill Atkinson's PhotoCard
$4.99

At this writing, the iPad has no camera. So Bill Atkinson's PhotoCard is almost reason enough to buy Apple's iPad Camera Connection Kit ($29; see Chapter 19), which lets you import photos and videos from most digital cameras via USB or SD card. And bring your iPad along any time you think you might shoot brilliant digital pictures.

Once you get your brilliant shots onto the iPad, you can touch them up and otherwise improve them with apps like Photogene and Adobe Photoshop Express (which are both discussed in Chapter 1). Or use one of the incredible Bill Atkinson shots (see the figure on the left below). When your image is awesome, use PhotoCard to send it to your friends and family via e-mail or the U.S. Postal Service with just a couple of taps.

I know I mentioned the quality of the printed cards sent via the USPS when I first mentioned PhotoCard back in Chapter 14, but let me say it again: The printed postcards are drop-dead gorgeous and are guaranteed to impress the recipient.

I'd also like to point out that PhotoCard is a hybrid app. It's not as easy to use on the smaller iPhone screen, but it is pretty convenient having this app on a device with a built-in camera.

The bottom line

If you're the postcard-sending type, you can't beat Bill Atkinson's PhotoCard for impressing your friends and family.

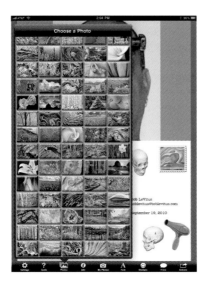

Atomic Web Browser
$0.99

I didn't have room in Chapter 15 for all the reasons I like this app. Please take another look at what I said about Atomic Web Browser there and review the figures. On the left is its best feature, tabbed browsing. On the right is its other best feature, full-screen browsing.

Let's start with the myriad of settings, including

- ✓ **Load on Startup:** Determine what you see when you launch the app — a bookmark folder, home page, last page viewed, last session (all open tabs), a blank page, or the option to choose the option at startup.

- ✓ **Identify Browser As:** Impersonate another Web browser, which can be useful if a site tells you it "requires Internet Explorer 6 or above." Atomic Browser can pretend to be that one, or several others as shown in the figure on the right below.

And I'm out of space again, without even mentioning great stuff like Privacy Options, Bookmark Scripts, Image Blocking, Rotation Lock (for specific pages), Autofill, Screen Dimmer, and even more.

The bottom line

Browse the Web much? The more you do, the more you'll appreciate Atomic Web Browser.

Improvox
$7.99

There are lots of apps that do interesting things with your voice —
including classics such as I Am T-Pain ($2.99) and Voice Changer HD
($0.99). Most are one-trick ponies. Many contain low-quality audio
effects. Some are in both those camps. Apps like that are banished
from my iPad within days.

Improvox's opening screen urges you to "Please put on your headphones," and that's good advice indeed. You'll get the best results
using an iPhone-style headset with a microphone.

It's fascinating to move the virtual joysticks, shown in the figure below
controlling All Harmonies (left joystick) and Stutter (right joystick).

I'd love to call myself a musician but that would be an insult to musicians. I do like to sing and play guitar, though I do neither very well.
I've made eight unedited recordings of me and my Improvox for you to
listen to or download. They are here: `http://www.dummies.com/go/`
`incredibleipadapps`.

The bottom line

Listen for yourself and I think you'll agree that Improvox is pretty darn
amazing.

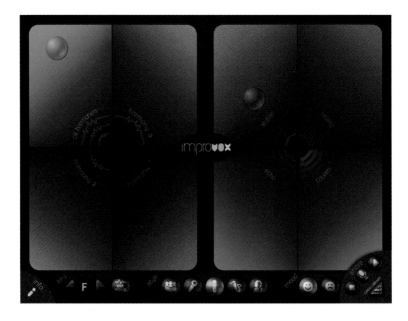

Instapaper
$4.99

As part of my daily ritual, I scan a dozen or more Web sites every morning for articles of interest. I often come across long articles that I'd like to read if I only had the time. So I use the handy Instapaper Read Later bookmark I've saved in Safari on my Mac and on my iPad, which adds the page to my unread items list in Instapaper and lets me get back to work.

Then, when I have downtime, I launch Instapaper and catch up on my reading. The great part is that I can read one or all of the articles, even when I have no network access whatsoever, as when I'm on an airplane, aboard a ship, or in a submarine.

That alone would be worth the price, but Instapaper also has a Graphical Pages setting that I turn off so that only the article's text is displayed, as shown in the figure on the left below. If I need to see the graphics, I click the View Original link at the top of the article; the original page appears in Instapaper's built-in Web browser, complete with ads, banners, and other graphics, as shown in the figure on the right.

The bottom line

Instapaper lets me save and read Web pages I might have skipped otherwise.

iTeleport
$24.99

Say I'm out to dinner with my wife when my iPhone begins to vibrate in my pocket. I take a peek at the screen surreptitiously and see an urgent text message from my editor:

Chapter 18 is missing and drop-deadline is in less than an hour! Please say you can send me the final draft of it right now. If you can't, our geese will be fricasseed.

So I launch iTelepad and, in seconds, I'm in control of my desktop Mac at home, commanding Microsoft Word to send the file to my editor as an attachment. My Mail program launches automatically and creates a message with the Word file enclosed. I quickly type a subject line and then click the Send Message button.

It took less than three minutes to avert that crisis.

The bottom line

iTeleport has saved my bacon (and my goose) more times than I care to count. It may seem expensive, but I've tried other iPhone virtual-network computing (VNC) apps, and none is as reliable or elegantly designed as iTeleport.

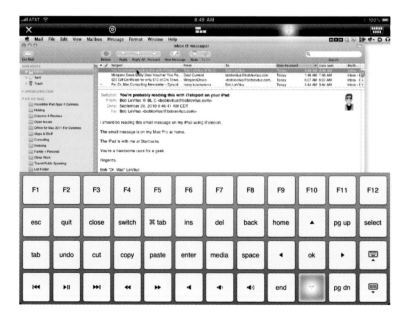

OmniGraffle
$49.99

Let me begin with some background: When Bryan and I were making our app picks for our chapters, OmniGraffle was the only app we were both adamant about keeping in our respective chapters. Bryan felt it was a business app and should be covered in his Chapter 3. I argued that it was a productivity app and should be covered in Chapter 11. We argued back and forth for a while.

"Business." "Productivity." "Business." "Productivity." "Business." "Productivity." We struck a compromise and included it in both chapters.

In Chapter 3, Bryan said, "If I had to pick just one company (outside of Apple) that I thought really grokked the iPad, it would have to be The Omni Group."

And in Chapter 11 I said it had "possibly the best user interface of any iPad app" and wished "other iPad apps I use regularly were as thoughtfully designed, powerful, and easy to use as OmniGraffle."

The bottom line

I admit the price sounds a little outrageous, but consider this: OmniGraffle for iPad lets you do much of what the OmniGraffle Mac application does — for half the price. So you could actually consider it a bargain.

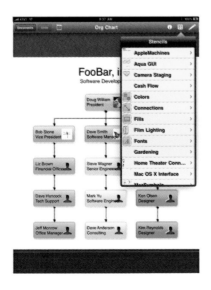

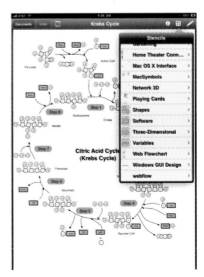

19 Ten Things That Make Your iPad Better

I spend a lot of time looking at iPhone, iPod, and iPad peripherals and accessories as a Reviews Editor for *The Mac Observer* (www.macobserver.com), my "Dr. Mac" column in *The Houston Chronicle*, and for my other writing gigs. In this chapter, I try to encapsulate everything I've learned from testing hundreds of accessories and products. Rest assured that the products I am about to recommend are ones I consider the best in their categories.

Apple Wireless Keyboard
$69

The Apple Wireless Keyboard is a way to use a top-notch aluminum physical keyboard without having to tether it to the iPad. It operates from up to 30 feet away from the iPad via Bluetooth, the wireless technology built into every one.

As with any Bluetooth device that the iPad makes nice with, you have to pair it to your iPad — generally a simple and straightforward process.

For me, placing the iPad in one of the stands I discuss later in the chapter and using a wireless keyboard with it is heavenly. I can work longer at writing — much longer — than if I used the touchscreen keyboard. It's more comfortable and, I suspect, more ergonomically correct as well.

The Apple Wireless Keyboard takes two AA batteries. It's smart about power management; it powers itself down when you stop using it to avoid draining those batteries. It wakes up again when you start typing.

It's very thin, so if you carry your iPad in a backpack, briefcase, messenger bag, or even a large purse, there's almost certainly enough room for an Apple Wireless Keyboard.

Though I haven't tested any, most non-Apple Bluetooth keyboards should work with your iPad, as long as the keyboard supports Bluetooth 2.1 + EDR technology.

Picture courtesy of Apple, Inc.

Car Accessories

Monster Cable iCarPlay iPod Cassette Adapter: $20
Griffin iTrip Auto SmartScan: $80
RadTech AutoPower: $10 – $17

If you're going to use your iPad in the car, here are a couple of handy devices to consider.

The first is a car audio adapter, a device that enables you to listen to music on your iPad through your car stereo system.

There are three main types of car audio adapters:

- ✔ **Auxiliary input:** If you have a car stereo system that includes a 3.5mm auxiliary input jack, you can buy a cable at Radio Shack for less than $10 and simply plug one end into the car stereo's input jack and the other end into your iPad's headphone jack. This setup offers the best possible sound quality but doesn't recharge your iPad.

- ✔ **Cassette adapter:** If your car stereo includes a cassette tape player, this is an excellent choice — it's inexpensive, it sounds better than an FM transmitter, and it's small and easy to conceal if you feel the need.

✔ **FM transmitter:** This type of car adapter broadcasts your iPad audio to your car's FM radio. Plug one into your iPad, tune your car radio to an unused frequency, and the music from your iPad comes out of your car stereo speakers. Sound quality ranges from decent to horrid and can change from minute to minute as you drive. An FM transmitter would be my last choice; but if your car stereo doesn't have a cassette player or auxiliary input jack, it may be your only option. If so, the Griffin iTrip Auto SmartScan is probably the best of the bunch.

The other device you should have, even if you don't want to *listen* to your iPad in the car, is a car charger. For that role, I recommend the RadTech AutoPower Vehicle Socket USB charger, available with one or two USB ports.

2-into-1 Stereo Adapter

A 2-into-1 stereo adapter is a handy little device that lets two people plug their headphones/earphones/headsets into one iPad (or iPod or iPhone for that matter). They're quite inexpensive (under $10) and extremely useful if you're traveling with a friend by air, sea, rail, or bus. They're also great when you want to watch a movie with your BFF but don't want to risk waking the neighbors or roommates.

I call 'em "2-into-1 stereo adapters," but that's not the only name they go by. Other names you might see for the same device are as follows:

✔ 3.5mm stereo Y-splitter

✔ ⅛-inch stereo 1-plug to 2-jacks adapter

✔ ⅛-inch stereo Y-adapter

✔ 3.5mm dual stereo headphone jack splitter

✔ And many others . . .

You really only need to know two things. The first thing: "⅛-inch" and "3.5mm" are used interchangeably in the adapter world (even though they're not really the same).

⅛ of an inch = 0.125 inch, whereas 3.5mm = 0.1378 inch. Not the same, but close enough for rock 'n' roll.

The second thing: You want to make sure that you get a *stereo* adapter. Some monaural adapters work but pump exactly the same sound into both ears, instead of sending the audio information for the left stereo channel to your left ear and the right stereo channel to your right.

In other words, you need a ⅛-inch or 3.5mm *stereo* adapter that has a single stereo plug on one end (to plug into your iPad) and two stereo jacks on the other end (to accommodate two sets of headphones/earphones/headsets).

iPad Camera Connection Kit
$29

The iPad doesn't include a USB port or SD memory card slot, which happen to be the most popular methods for getting pictures from a digital camera onto a computer. As you know by now, the iPad also lacks its own camera (as of this writing).

All the same, the iPad delivers a marvelous photo viewer. That's why, if you take a lot of pictures, Apple's $29 iPad Camera Connection Kit is worth considering. It consists of two components, as shown in the figure below.

Either of these components plugs into the 30-pin connector at the bottom of the iPad. One sports a USB interface that you can use with the USB cable that came with your camera to download pix. The other is an SD Card Reader that lets you insert the memory card that stores your pictures.

Home Speakers
Blue Sky EXO2: $499
Audioengine 2: $200
Bose Companion II: $100

There isn't a speaker system yet that I know of that's built specifically for the iPad. Instead, most people plug iPads into self-powered speaker systems or home theater systems. I'll get to video later in this chapter — but for now, bear in mind that you can use your existing A/V Receiver, portable speaker system, powered speaker system, wireless speaker system, iPod or iPhone alarm clock, or other audio devices with your iPad. All you need is the right cable — ⅛-inch or 3.5mm stereo adapter on one end and whatever your A/V Receiver or powered speaker system needs on the other end — and you can probably find a suitable cable at Radio Shack for under $10.

That said, here are three powered speaker systems that I consider good values at their price points.

- ✔ **Blue Sky EXO2:** I'm currently partial to Blue Sky's EXO2 system. With a thumping 8-inch sealed-box subwoofer, this 2.1 desktop speaker system kicks butt. It's not cheap (around $450 on the street), but it's billed as a "complete stereo monitoring system" and that's just what it is. The rich, accurate reproduction at all levels and tight, bone-jarring bass always make me smile.

   But I agree, that's a lot of dough for (another) set of speakers. For those who would prefer to spend less, here are two more options:

- ✔ **Audioengine 2:** These self-powered desktop speakers are designed to work with pretty much any audio device, including your computer (which is where many people put them to work) and are optimized to reproduce digital audio from MP3, AAC, WAV, and so on. They are, simply put, the best $200 speakers I have heard to date (and believe me, I've heard a lot of speakers).

   Enough said.

- ✔ **Bose Companion 2 Series II:** These are the only ones I've not used extensively in my home or office. But I've heard them a few times in different settings and am impressed at how good they sounded for a hundred bucks. I've always considered Bose products overpriced and unspectacular but these particular speakers are at least one exception.

Travel Speakers
iMainGo2: $40
Altec-Lansing Orbit MP3: $50

I like to have music available at all times, and I don't like earphones if I can avoid them. So I've tested lots of travel speakers over the years. You can't go wrong with either of these:

- ✔ **iMainGo2:** This is actually a combination iPhone/iPod case and high-performance speaker — but it works great with the iPad too. In my 5-star (out of 5) review of the original iMainGo, I said, "With

its reasonable price tag, tiny size, huge sound, and quality construction, iMainGo is without a doubt the best ultra-portable iPod
speaker system I've seen to date. Or, as my 18-year-old daughter
puts it, 'That thing is soooo tight!'" The iMainGo2 looks pretty
much the same — but sounds better than the original and costs
$20 less.

✔ **Orbit:** The Altec-Lansing Orbit MP3 is smaller than the iMainGo2
but it still sounds great. This little gem runs for days on three AAA
batteries, has a nice little protective case, plus handy wraparound
cable storage. The only downside is that it's a single speaker so
you hear mono instead of stereo. On the other hand, it's darn *good-*
sounding mono, which may be perfectly acceptable.

Wired Headphones, Earphones, and Headsets

Grado SR60i: $99
Klipsch Image S4 Headphones: $79
Klipsch Image S4i In-Ear Headset with Mic and Remote: $99

You've surely noticed that your iPad did not include earphones or a
headset. That's probably a blessing because the earphones and headsets Apple has included with iPods and iPhones since time immemo-
rial aren't all that good. In fact, I have referred to them as, "mediocre
and somewhat uncomfortable" in almost every article I've ever written
about the iPod or iPhone.

Search Amazon.com for headphones, earphones, or headsets and
you'll find that thousands of each are available at prices ranging from
around $10 to over $1,000. Or, if you prefer to shop in a brick-and-
mortar store, Target, Best Buy, and the Apple Store all have decent
selections, with prices starting at less than $20.

Much as I love the shopping experience at Apple Stores, you won't
find any bargains there. Bargain-hunting doesn't matter that much for
Apple-branded products, because they're rarely discounted. However,
you can almost always find widely available non-Apple items such as
headphones, earphones, and headsets cheaper somewhere else.

With so many brands and models of earphones, headphones, and
headsets available from so many manufacturers at so many price
points, I can't possibly test even a fraction of the ones available today.
That said, I've probably tested more of them than most people — and
I definitely have my favorites.

Earphones? Headphones? Headsets?

I have referred to headphones and headsets several times, and thought you might be wondering whether there's a difference — and if so, what it is. When I talk about *headphones* or *earphones*, I'm talking about the things you use to listen to music. A *headset* adds a microphone so you can use it for voice chatting, recording voice notes, and (in the case of the iPhone or Internet VOIP services such as Skype) for phone calls. So headphones and earphones are for listening, and headsets are for both talking and listening.

Now, you may be wondering whether earphones and headphones are the same. To some people they may be, but to us, headphones (shown on the left below) have a band across the top (or back) of your head, and the listening apparatus is big and covers the outside of your ears. Think of the big fat things you see covering a radio

disk jockey's ears. Earphones (sometimes referred to as *earbuds* and shown on the right in the figure), on the other hand, are smaller, fit entirely in your ear, and have no band across the top or back of your head.

Headsets can be earphone style or, less commonly, headphone style. The distinguishing factor is that headsets always include a microphone. And some headsets are designed specifically for use with Apple i-products (iPhone, iPod, iPad) and have integrated Play/Pause and volume control buttons.

One last thing: Some companies refer to their earbud products as headphones, but I think that's confusing and wrong. So in this book, *headphones* are those bulky, outside-the-ear things and *earphones* are teeny-tiny things that fit entirely in your ear canal.

When it comes to headphones, I'm partial to my Grado SR60i's, which are legendary for offering astonishingly accurate audio at an affordable price (around $80 street). I've tried headphones that cost twice, thrice, or even more times as much that I didn't think sounded nearly as good.

For earphones and earphone-style headsets, I like the Klipsch Image S4 Headphones and S4i In-Ear Headset with Mic and 3-Button Remote. At around $79 and $99, respectively, they sound better than many similarly priced products and better than many more expensive offerings.

Protective Cases

iFrogz Silicone Wrapz and Luxe Original iPad cases: $29.99 and $39.99
iSkin Duo and Vu iPad cases: $49.99 and $64.99
RadTech Gelz and Aero iPad cases: $24.95 and $29.95

The iPad is surprisingly resistant to scratches and dings, but I still feel better with something protecting mine. I've tested dozens of 'em; here are some of my favorite cases, from companies I can recommend without hesitation:

✔ **iFrogz Silicone Wrapz and Luxe Original:** I love the iFrogz Silicone Wrapz and Luxe Original cases. The Luxe Original is my favorite, a two-piece hardshell case with a beautiful colored finish on the top piece and flat black on the bottom. It looks great and feels great in your hands. The iFrogz Silicone Wrapz is flexible, rubbery, one-piece silicone case that also feels pretty nice to the touch. I think both of these cases make your iPad feel a little less slippery The Luxe Original comes in Blue, Iron, Orange, Pink, Red, and Teal; the Silicone Wrapz comes in Black, Red, White, Blue, and Pink. I have a lot of friends who love these ultra-thin, lightweight cases, and I'm sure you will too.

✔ **iSkin Duo and Vu:** I also love the iSkin brand cases. They seem to be a tad better-looking than others, and include thoughtful extras like the removable docking hatch on the Vu for protecting the charging port or the covered and protected volume button, power button, and earphone jack on both models.

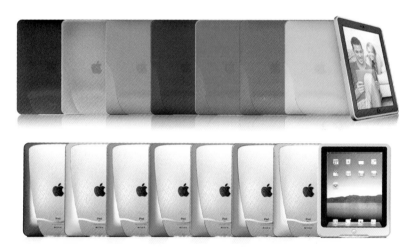

Courtesy of iSkin

✔ **RadTech Gelz and Aero:** The RadTech products are similar to the iFrogz designs. They're well made and less expensive than the other brands.

Never spray anything directly onto the screen of your iPad (or of any other electronic device). Always spray it onto a cloth, preferably microfiber, and use that to clean the screen.

Stands

LapDesk iPad Recliner: $44.95
Griffin A-Frame: $49.99
Classic Woods 8-inch (20cm) walnut finish easel: $6/99

✔ **iPad Recliner:** I really like the iPad Recliner from LapWorks. The viewing angle is pretty much infinitely adjustable, and the soft rubber cushions play nice with your iPad. And unlike some stands, the iPad Recliner works with most third-party cases.

✔ **A-Frame:** The A-Frame is so unusual I just had to include it. As you can see in the figure below, it's a dual-purpose desktop stand made of heavy-duty aluminum. You can open it to hold your iPad in either portrait or landscape mode for watching video, displaying pictures (a great way to exploit the Picture Frame mode), or even for reading. In this upright mode, it's also the perfect companion for the Apple Wireless Keyboard (or any other Bluetooth keyboard for that matter). Or, if you close the legs and lay it down, it puts your iPad at the perfect angle for using the onscreen keyboard.

Soft silicone padding keeps your iPad from getting scratched or sliding around, and the bottom lip is designed to accommodate the charging cable in portrait mode. Furthermore, like the iPad Recliner, it works with third-party cases, including Griffin's own flexible and hardshell cases.

I like this thing; it's where my iPad resides pretty much any time it's not in my backpack.

✔ **Classic Woods 8-inch (20cm) walnut finish easel:** Okay. I agree that 50 bucks is a lot of scratch for a simple iPad stand. And so, gentle reader, on your behalf I went to Michael's (arts and crafts store) to investigate some really cheap iPad stands that fellow author Andy Ihnatko had mentioned. What I found at Michaels were easels intended to display framed artwork or decorative plates on a tabletop. There were several plastic and wood easels that worked beautifully with the iPad in either portrait and landscape mode, but the one I liked best was, "Classic Woods 8-inch (20cm) Walnut Finish Easel," priced at $6.99.

Video output to TV

iPad Dock Connector to VGA Adapter cable: $29
Apple Composite AV Cable: $49
Apple Component AV Cable: $49

The iPad has a pretty big screen for what it is, a tablet computer. But that display is still not nearly as large as a living room TV or a monitor you might see in a conference room or auditorium.

Projecting what's on the iPad's 1024 x 768 screen to a larger display is the very reason behind the iPad Dock Connector to VGA Adapter cable that Apple sells for $29. You can use it to connect your iPad to computer displays, projectors, televisions, or any other device with a VGA input. In a nutshell, it allows you to watch videos, slideshows, and presentations on bigger screens.

Or, if you have a TV that has no VGA port but does have either a Component or Composite video input, Apple has a cable for that as well. These cables also work with your iPhone and iPod in addition to your iPad — and come with a power supply that includes a USB port so you can charge your device while you watch its content on a big-screen TV.

 Some early buyers of these cables have been disappointed, however, because the product doesn't exactly mirror the iPad (iPhone/iPod) display at all times. In fact, it all-too-frequently doesn't. The app you're using has to support playing video to an external display — and not that many do. Among those I know of that do are:

✔ Videos, Photos, and YouTube among the iPad's built-in apps

✔ The $9.99 Apple Keynote app

✔ Safari, which works for some videos, but not everything you're viewing through the browser

By the way, because of digital rights restrictions, you may not be able to display movies you buy from the iTunes Store if you're using these cables.

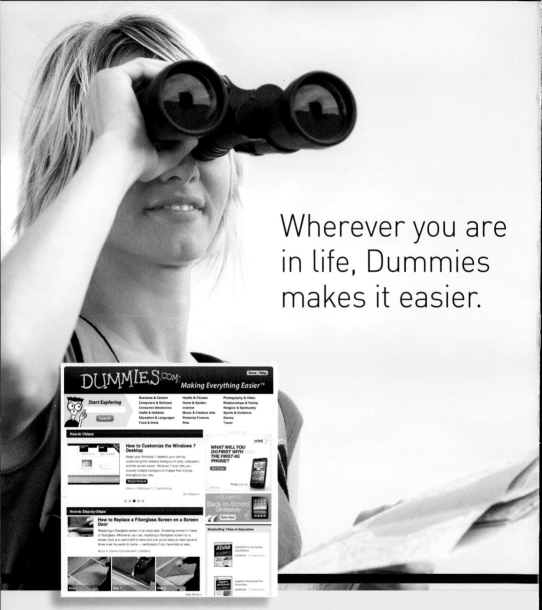